KACHEMAK BAY
COMMUNITIES

Their Histories, Their Mysteries

Janet Klein

KACHEMAK BAY COMMUNITIES
THEIR HISTORIES, THEIR MYSTERIES

Janet R. Klein

Kachemak Country Publications
Homer, Alaska

To

Phil, Linda and Kay,

especially Kay whose fine drawings

enhance this book.

Edited by Penny Rennick

Library of Congress Card Number 2008933821
Printed in the United States of America
17 16 15 14 13 12 11 10 09 08   1 2 3 4 5

Published by
Kachemak Country Publications
PO Box 2386
Homer, Alaska 99603

ISBN—978-0-9651157-4-2

Cover design: Rachel Gebauer
Text layout and design: Mary Maly
Cover image: Steve Baird, Kachemak Bay Research Reserve. Based
on data from U.S. Geological Survey.

For the purpose of this book, the mouth of Kachemak Bay extends
along an imaginary line between Anchor Point and Nanwalek.

TABLE OF CONTENTS

ACKNOWLEDGMENTS

Many people contributed to this publication. It benefited greatly from the assistance of friends and professionals who know Kachemak Country or have specialized knowledge that helped me better interpret it. Thank you Margaret Anderson, Game McGimsey, Marilyn Knapp, Gretchen Abbott Bersch, Maren Anderson, Steve Smith, Karen Workman, David McMahan, Rick Bilak, Michael Armstrong, Peter Zollars, Bruce Merrell, Bill Workman, Helen Alm, Peter Haeussler and Findlay Abbott. Hopefully, I have accurately interpreted what you shared with me; however, any mistakes are mine. Jill Fredson and Stephen Haycox granted permission to include a quotation from their writings. Penny Rennick, who edited these pages, made my writing more professional while Mary Maly created the attractive layout and design.

In 2002 I enjoyed a wonderful research trip to Europe. Dr. Peter Bolz at the Ethnologisches Museum Berlin provided objects from Tyonek, Kenai and Soonroodna, a former Native village in Kachemak Bay, for me to study. Martin Franken and Dietrich Graf photographed many objects for the first time since they were collected in 1883. Pam Woolliscroft at the Spode Museum in central England, trusted me to leaf through tomes containing the original drawings of earthenware patterns from the 1800s; and, during a fine dinner with John and Pat Lilley, I learned that John had attended school with members of the Hesketh family. The picture of Sir Thomas Hesketh was obtained with his help.

Illustrations enhance many pages. Some photographs such as those taken by William Wakeland are of professional quality; others are from family scrapbooks. Even though a few are over a century old and show their age, I am delighted to include them and thank the families of Sarah Eldred, Homer Pennock, Sir Thomas Hesketh and others who shared them so willingly. Drawings by Gary Lyon, Lee Post and Kay VanDervoort help interpret this history. It was especially fun working with Kay, my talented sister, who lived in Homer for all too-short-of-a-time. Dick Hanscom, author of *Alaska and Yukon Stocks and Bonds*, donated the use of the images of the stock certificates. Betsy Webb, at the Pratt Museum, Homer, always provided information and images quickly and professionally as did Kathleen Hertel and Tracy Leithauser at the Anchorage Museum. Contemporary photographs with no credit line were taken by me.

My personal interests and the availability of images and information dictated what was included in this book. I remain fascinated with not only what is known of Kachemak Country but with what remains to be learned.

First Thoughts

The stories of Kachemak Country are as fascinating and varied as its people, wildlife and land. This land has been occupied by people for over 8,000 years. We walk in their footsteps, camp where they camped, harvest the same species they harvested, build our homes atop their ancient home sites and boat where they boated. The waters of Kachemak Bay provided food, served as an aquatic road system and inspired creative expression to them and now to us.

The history of our region is relatively young if we define history as that time when people first wrote about their observations. Captain James Cook penned observations in his ship's log as he sailed up the adjacent inlet in 1778. (Cook did not sail into Kachemak Bay.) Although earlier information about Kachemak Bay may exist in Russian documents, that information has yet to reach us.

History is fluid, open to new and fresh interpretations as information becomes available. Each of us interprets our own experiences through our own biases and knowledge. Personal stories, such as Steve Zawistowski's experience raising foxes, belong to the individual. While his activities reflect those of other fox farmers, his story is unique.

The initial explorations into the natural and cultural histories of Kachemak Country were carried out by agriculturalists and archaeologists, biologists and botanists, cartographers, ethnographers, geologists, itinerant priests and others. Usually, these travelers visited briefly in summer when the land was lush and lovely and wildlife existed in profusion. All returned to their respective states or foreign countries taking their new-found knowledge and, often, objects and photographs. A few men, however, came to develop get-rich-quick schemes. They created ephemeral communities then sold stock in their bogus ventures. These were the con men of Kachemak Country.

The stories of these adventurers are found in ships' logs, scientific papers, church records, journals, family archives and American and foreign repositories. A fading photograph, an aging document, a map, even a place name can tell a story, reveal a fresh perspective or correct erroneous information. Publications and photographs unavailable in 1981 when I wrote *A History of Kachemak Bay, the Country, the Communities*, have allowed me to update and make corrections to information from that book. Several chapters from *A History. . .* are included in this publication; however, each incorporates new material. Some stories, such as those about Aurora and Soonroodna, are told in greater detail primarily because substantial new information was found.

This book opens with an overview of Kachemak geology and physical geography then builds the foundation for our history with a timeline of major European and Russian activities and finally details select events from the 1800s into the mid-1900s. Because the earthquake of 1964 irreparably changed the character of several Kachemak communities, that catastrophe is described briefly.

Regardless of what new information and images have been uncovered, there will always be an indefinable essence, an aura of mystery, that is pure Kachemak. And that's as it should be.

"We remember a place not just for its beauty but for the way that beauty made us feel; those feelings are woven into the emotional tapestry we call self. The most special places are the ones that give texture to our dreams, that ground us, make us whole, remind us of what is real."

Jill Fredston
Rowing to Latitude, Journeys Along the Arctic's Edge

"Knowing the history of a particular place, especially the place where one lives, can create a sense of identity with that place, and with the people of that place. Realizing that we tread the same ground that others before us trod, and that we live today with the results of the decisions those people made, can greatly strengthen our sense of commonality. People come to feel they are participants in the same drama, the same story. But only if we remember."

Stephen Haycox
"Looking to past can help today"
Anchorage Daily News

THE SHAPE OF KACHEMAK COUNTRY

Geology, the science that deals with the origin and history of the earth, its formations and the changes they undergo, is a powerful and dynamic discipline in Kachemak Country. Complex forces created, shaped and continue to shape this land. This chapter presents simplified explanations of some of those forces. These are the stories in stone, read in the lay of the land and in the folds of a rock formation, gleaned from the grinding movements of glaciers and found in the fossilized remains of plants and fish. Most stories speak of a distant time and a colder or warmer clime.

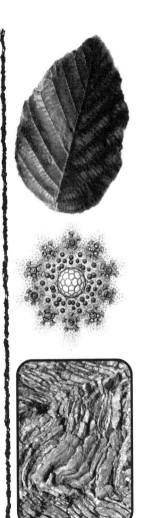

The Kachemak watershed encompasses fresh, glacial and salt waters, sandspits and sandstone bluffs, lowland hills and upland plateaus, mountains, glaciers, islands and deep aquatic canyons. Most geographic features are unnamed, many valleys unexplored, mountains and ridges unclimbed, glaciers untrod; probably though, every bay, cove, lagoon and shoreline has been diligently and repeatedly explored for people fished, hunted, gathered, traveled and dwelled along these waterways. Although they hunted wildlife and, more recently, minerals in the high country, most people lived along the coast and traveled upon bay waters, as they do today.

KACHEMAK TRIPTYCH

Kachemak Country is a triptych where three separate, adjacent entities—mountains, water, hills—coalesce to create one striking environment. Each entity is enhanced by the other two; combined, they are more diverse, dynamic and stunning than any one single element.

The beauty of this land is legendary. This country of contrasts delights the eye, stimulates the senses and intrigues the mind.

Taken from atop the inland bluff after 1945, this photograph shows the low-lying Homer benchland, the Homer Spit and the distant Kenai Mountains. Each component of the triptych, the mountains, the bay and the benchlands and hills, has its own geology and geography, plant and animal life, climate and even its own history. These disparities make Kachemak Bay unique. *Steve McCutcheon Collection, Anchorage Museum*

2

SOUTH SHORE

The Kenai Mountains, which comprise what many residents call the south shore, curl like a protective arm along the eastern and southern shoreline of Kachemak Bay. Sea-to-sky-scraping peaks deflect many harsh winter storms originating in the North Pacific Ocean and temper the climate. Deeply indented bays and fjords, rocky headlands and islands, fertile estuaries, glacial outwash plains and numerous spits characterize this coast. Geologically, a spit is a long narrow strip of unconsolidated materials such as sand and gravel formed by the transportation and deposition of those sediments by water. Major spits along the south shore include Aurora, Glacier, MacDonald and the unnamed spit protecting China Poot Bay. McKeon Spit, which once protected much of Neptune Bay, has eroded so much that it has almost disappeared.

U.S. Geological Survey Landsat 7

The mountains reveal countless stories in stone. Formed between 245-100 million years ago during the Triassic, Jurassic and Early Cretaceous Periods, they are geologically complex. Older rocks, mostly buried deep beneath the surface, were formed during the Permian Period 286-245 million years ago and are exposed around Nanwalek and Port Graham.

Meltwater from the high country flows into lakes, cascades into creeks, then rushes into and enriches Kachemak Bay.

Toby Wheeler, Homer geologist, inspects slate from the narrow outcrop behind him in 1991. Today, that outcrop is under Bradley Lake.

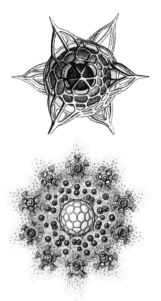

The bedrock of much of this shore is exotic—originating far south of Alaska as part of an ancient oceanic plate. Sedimentary and volcanic rock types such as graywacke, basalt, pillow basalt, argillite, tuff, chert and radiolarian chert can be seen along the coast. Some rocks were scraped off of sea mounts and moved northward over time.

Radiolaria

4

Radiolarian chert, below, outcrops along the south shore. Millions of years ago in tropical and near-tropical oceanic waters, unfathomable numbers of miniscule one-celled animals called radiolaria lived and died. Their complex and often spiky silicate exoskeletons accumulated on the deep ocean floor. Over time and under pressure, the radiolarian ooze was compressed into rock known as radiolarian chert. Later, the gray, green, black and red radiolarian cherts were pressured into great folds, pleats and chevrons.

Less common rocks of the south shore include limestone and marble exposed at Gray Cliff near Seldovia, greenish serpentinite occasionally found as glacially rounded rocks in the Wosnesenski River valley and chromite-bearing rocks at Red Mountain and Snow Prospect. Chromite, rare in the other states, was mined at Port Chatham, south of Nanwalek, during World War I and at Red Mountain, southeast of Seldovia, from 1942 to 1944 and 1954 to 1957. Snow Prospect, near the head of Seldovia Bay, is a relatively new site and a new place name for Kachemak Bay. The chromite there had not been mined as of 2007.

This photograph, taken in the 1950s, shows a holding crib in Kasitsna Bay where ore from Red Mountain was stockpiled. When a transport ship anchored alongside the deep-water dock, the ore was delivered to its hold on the conveyor belt alongside the dock.

While there's gold on the Kenai Peninsula, along the north shore of Kachemak Bay it is likely to be finely scattered placer gold such as that sluiced in the Anchor River in the 1890s. The source of that gold may be the Kenai Mountains or from glacially deposited

Richard W. Tyler Historic Photograph Collection, PM-2001-14-25, Pratt Museum

materials. Lode gold was mined along the outer Pacific coast near Nuka Bay between 1920 and 1940.

Glaciers gave shape to Kachemak Country—defining the present topography of both shores and even the shape of the floor of Kachemak Bay. Today, those vast land-shapers are gone from the north shore and reduced to remnant glaciers in the Kenai Mountains.

Grewingk, a prominent glacier seen from the north shore, was named for Constantin Grewingk who, although he never visited Alaska, wrote a book about the geology and volcanology of Alaska when it was a Russian colony. The names of other glaciers honor European and Russian navigators, scientists and explorers such as Dinglestadt, Dixon, Doroshin, Portlock and Wosnesenski.

Glacial ice is unique. Over vast spans of time and during long periods of cold, snow amassed in the Kenai Mountains. As the snow depth and weight increased, each single flake metamorphosed into an ice crystal. Combined, the crystals formed glacial ice.

Eventually, their weight and pressure forced great fingers of ice to flow downhill shaping the land as they moved.

During the Pleistocene Epoch, which lasted from about 1.8 million years ago to 10,000 years ago, periods of warmth alternated with periods of cold. During the cold, great ice fields draped across the crest of the Kenai Mountains and filled adjacent valleys. Simultaneously, great sheet glaciers weighed heavily upon the non-mountainous area of the Kenai Peninsula. During ". . .the most extensive glaciation recorded in the Cook Inlet region, icecaps blanketed the surrounding Alaska Range and the Talkeetna, Chugach, and Kenai Mountains, and completely filled Cook Inlet to elevations above 4,000 feet," according to Thor Karlstrom, geologist.

Grewingk Glacier was melting when measured by William H. Dall in 1880, 1895 and 1899. The three men, standing on the glacial tongue in 1895, provide scale. Gravel, transported by the ice, dirties its surface. In 2008, the glacier was one-and-a-half to two miles farther east than it is in this photograph. *Purington, C. W. 55. U.S. Geological Survey; PM-2003-22-2, Pratt Museum*

As glacial ice advanced and retreated, it scratched, smoothed or rounded softer rocks, polished harder ones and transported pebbles, gravel and sizeable boulders from one place to another. The great ice-gougers contoured the bedrock and sculpted features such as English, Seldovia and Tutka Bays and Sadie and Bear Coves. Sadie Cove, with its U-shaped profile and marine water cupped between steep-sided mountains, is a classic fjord. The cove is 330-feet deep at its mouth, 204-feet deep about mid-cove and still 180-feet deep near the shallow end. Eight-mile-long Tutka Bay, adjacent to Sadie Cove, is another glacial canyon. The word, "Tutka," is derived from a Dena'ina word meaning 'big enclosure.' W.H. Dall, who named many features in Kachemak Bay, recorded that name in 1880.

Not many decades ago the Harding Icefield, in the mountains north and east of Homer, was about the size of Rhode Island, 1,100 square miles. Over 38 glaciers flowed from it, some toward Kachemak Bay, some toward the Gulf of Alaska. Since 1973 the Harding Icefield has shrunk considerably and a smaller second field now exists: the Grewingk-Yalik. Today, although fewer than a dozen named and several smaller unnamed glaciers flow toward Kachemak Bay, none reach the sea. The shrinking of the local glaciers is attributed to climate change.

Sadie Peak, the highest in the southern Kenai Mountains, rises 4,320 feet above the China Poot Bay estuary.

Another fascinating feature of the south shore is its estuaries, areas where fresh water mixes with salt water. Nutrient-rich estuaries serve as nursery grounds for shellfish, fish and for some of the 450 species of invertebrates which live in Kachemak Bay.

Seldovia is the largest community on the south shore with slightly fewer than 300 city residents in 2005. An excellent location on Seldovia Bay allowed for the development of fur trading during the Russian occupation and the development of commercial fisheries during the American period. From the late 1800s until the mid-twentieth century, Seldovia was the major seaport for steamships and for passengers traveling throughout Southcentral Alaska. *Tom and Mary Glover*

BAY WATERS

The very heart of the triptych is Kachemak Bay itself—the waters that separate, yet unite, the disparate shores. At the mouth of the bay are three historic communities: Anchor Point to the north, Port Graham and Nanwalek to the south. Although the softly contoured hills around Anchor Point contrast sharply with the mountains backing Nanwalek and Port Graham, the communities share a sea-oriented heritage.

Kachemak Bay trends northeastward from its mouth for about 38 miles to end at the Fox River Flats, an extensive tidal estuary drained by braided freshwater streams. The coastline of the bay extends for about 320 miles.

The tides generate a daily rhythm of relatively predictable water levels. Twice every 24 hours and 50 minutes the tide is high and twice it is low. The height of the tide is influenced by phases of the moon, its proximity to and alignment with the earth and sun, underwater contours of the bay and other factors. In 2008 the highest tide was a plus twenty-two feet, two inches (+22.2) above sea level in November; the lowest was a minus five feet, seven inches (−5.7) below sea level in June. These extremes vary through the years. A strong low pressure system can push the water inches higher. Several weeks a month, when the sun, moon and earth are not in alignment, the variation between the high and low tides is minimal, often only six to eight feet. The tides also influence where people live and how they build their structures. Boating, fishing, beach hiking, camping and other activities are scheduled around the tides. The annual tide book is critical to living and playing safely along the shores of Kachemak Bay.

The land and waters of Kachemak Bay are bird-rich. With its varied ecosystems, relatively mild seasons and abundant food, the bay attracts many bird species year around such as bald eagles, loons and chickadees. Two hundred forty-eight species have been recorded. Of those, about half are aquatic-associated species—seabirds, waterfowl and shorebirds. Every spring, the estuaries and tidal flats serve as major resting and feeding areas for thousands of migrating birds. During summer, rocky headlands and rugged sea stacks such as Sixty-foot Rock and those of the Gull Island

Steller's jay. *Drawing by Wanda Seamster*

rookery provide habitat for nesting seabirds such as tufted and horned puffins, black-legged kittiwakes, common murres and cormorants. Bald eagles soar above the rookeries, finding prey easily and in abundance. In winter, as many as 68 species have been recorded by participants in the annual Audubon Christmas Bird Count.

Raven. *Drawing by Lee Post*

Deep in winter, ice forms in the freshwater streams of the Fox River Flats. Often, it is carried on the tides or pushed by north winds downbay to jam against the Homer Spit. Occasionally, salt water freezes and ice fills the Homer Small Boat Harbor as it did in the winter of 2007–2008.

Much of Kachemak Bay, however, remains ice-free, in part, because the Kuroshio (Japanese) Current crosses the Pacific Ocean then strikes the West Coast of North America. From there, two currents swing northward: the Alaska Current and, nearer shore, the Alaska Coastal Current. Flowing across the Gulf of Alaska and entering Cook Inlet, this lower-salinity water helps moderate the climate of Kachemak Bay.

A variety of habitats creates a lengthy and complex food web for aquatic animals ranging from microscopic zooplankton to quarter-inch-long pteropods, tiny winged snails, to 35 to 40 ton humpback whales. At least 15 species of marine mammals have been documented locally. While harbor seals, sea otters and Steller's sea lions are permanent residents, others such as a live walrus and northern fur seal and carcasses of northern elephant seals and Bering Sea beaked whales, are not. Changes in water temperatures are accompanied, occasionally, by changes in marine life.

Humpback whales. *Drawing by Gary Lyon*

The tides and currents occasionally deliver other unexpected objects: a green sea turtle, seaweeds and cedar logs from Southeast Alaska and crude oil from the 1989 wreck of the *Exxon Valdez*

11

tanker in Prince William Sound.

The importance of the marine life and relatively clean waters of Kachemak Bay is recognized in its status as a state critical habitat area and also as a National Estuarine Research Reserve. Designated in 1999, the reserve encompasses approximately 365,000 acres of land and water and is the only fjord-type estuary in the U.S. Research Reserve System.

The waters of Kachemak Bay which form the very heart of the triptych reflect and magnify the beauty of the south shore mountains and the north shore hills.

NORTH SHORE

The north shore, as defined by many residents, consists of the Homer Spit, a low benchland upon which are situated Homer and Kachemak City and an inland bluff wrinkled with canyons vegetated with cottonwood and shrubs. The bluff gives way to hills which rise to 1,622–foot high Lookout Mountain and to the higher Boxcar and Caribou Hills. Creeks such as Diamond, McNeil, Fritz, Fox, Twitter and Swift, along with the Anchor River, originate is this high country. Spruce, birch and cottonwood grow among extensive areas of muskeg and meadow.

U.S. Geological Survey, Landsat 7

The rivers which braid across the Fox River Flats spring from montane glaciers such as Chernof, Kachemak and Dinglestadt. Vegetation on the flats is primarily marsh grass.

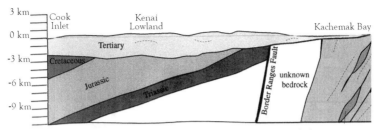

A geologic cross section shows the stratigraphy of the Kenai Lowland, the Border Ranges Fault and the bedrock of a portion of the Kenai Mountains. *U.S. Geological Survey, Geologic Map of the Seldovia Quadrangle*

The stories in stone on the north shore reveal origins far different from those of the south shore. During the geologically recent Tertiary and Quaternary Periods, 65 million years ago to the present, over one-and-one-fourth miles of sandstone, shale, peat, coal and volcanic ash were deposited repeatedly atop the bedrock. Layers of these materials are visible in the sea bluffs from the Fox River Flats to Anchor Point and beyond. Streams meandered across the land as evidenced in ripple-marked siltstones and mudstones.

On the north shore and, to a far lesser extent, on the south shore, plants of many species thrived, died and were preserved as fossil leaves, twigs, branches, trunks and even cones. These plants are divided into types. Two types were identified and named from specimens collected near Seldovia, Coal Cove in Port Graham and Homer. The Seldovian–type specimens represent plants which grew in a warm temperature environment such as *Ginkgo biloba*, oak, elm and maple. The Homerian flora represents species which thrived in a cool temperate environment such as willows, poplars, birches, roses and rhododendrons.

Metasequoia, an ancestor to the giant redwood or Sequoia of the Pacific

Fossilized alder leaves

Northwest, grew in both environments. Terrestrial plants were converted, occasionally, into coal and peat while in the seas marine plants were converted into petroleum and gas.

The presence of coal fueled numerous economic enterprises. On the south shore, where coal is not common, one of the longest operating businesses was run by William Whorf who came to Kachemak Country around 1894. He reopened the Russian mine at Coal Cove on Port Graham waterway, obtained patent to the property and sold coal to passing ships. Near Homer, the mines near Bidarka Creek were worked from 1899 to 1902, from 1915 to 1923 and then again from World War II to about 1950.

The abundance of plant fossils belies the scarcity of animal fossils. An enduring mystery confounding scientists exploring much of Alaska, including Kachemak Bay, is: Where are the fossilized remains or imprints of the vertebrate animals that inhabited this land during the Tertiary Period? In 1960, 1961 and 1963, John A. Dorr, Jr. and others examined the sea bluffs from near Stone Steps Lake, east of Homer, to Anchor Point, a distance of about 30 miles. They also surveyed rock exposures in McNeil, Thurston, Waterman and Bear Canyons and roadcuts around Homer. According to Dorr, "Not a single fragment was found of fossilized vertebrate bone of non-marine origin and pre-Pleistocene age in the Tertiary of Alaska." Fossilized vertebrates were, and still are, missing not only in Kachemak Bay but throughout much of Alaska!

Dorr's explanations for the failure to locate any such fossils included their destruction by ground movement, the normal rarity of fossil vertebrates, low population densities of animals during the Tertiary, unfavorable depositional environments, insufficient search and bad luck. He wrote that the later two reasons ". . . are probably the most likely. . . " causes for not locating Tertiary fossils.

Presently, the only vertebrate fossils reported locally are those of fish. In 1962, Marion Johnson of Spenard, Alaska, found one-half of a concretion containing three fossil fish near Bidarka Creek, west of Homer. They were tentatively identified at the U.S. National Museum (today National Museum of Natural History, Washington, D.C.) as a trout-perch or pirate perch. The concretion was sent to a repository in Fairbanks but its whereabouts was unknown in 2008. Robert James, of Homer, found the other half of the trout-perch concretion and donated it to the Pratt Museum where it remains. In the 1990s, Don Triplehorn, a Fairbanks scientist, discovered a cluster of unidentified fossilized fish near Seldovia. They were not *in situ*, not in the place where they were deposited originally and, thus, could not be dated. Another Fairbanks scientist, Stuart Rawlinson, however, found fossilized sticklebacks ranging from seven-to-eight million years of age near McNeil Canyon.

Triplehorn sought vertebrate fossils throughout Kachemak Bay and elsewhere in the State. "Tertiary vertebrates are scarce and I have spent some time looking for them. Tons of stuff in the Pleistocene and a fair amount (mainly dinosaurs) in the Cretaceous, but nothing [in] between. [It's a] big mystery."

A MAMMOTH MYSTERY

Mammoth. *Drawing by Kay VanDervoort*

The woolly mammoth was adopted as Alaska's state fossil in 1986. Mature mammoths, with their pronounced foreheads, sloping backs and thick coats, had 12-foot-long tusks and stood 9 to 10-feet-tall at the shoulder.

During glacial intervals late in the Pleistocene Epoch, animals such as camels, horses, lions, steppe bison and woolly mammoths roamed the cold, arid arctic grassland extending across northern Eurasia, Alaska and Canada. Mammoths were an integral part of the ecosystem and their tusks and bones have been found in many locations, particularly in ancient river banks or washed out of the permafrost in central Alaska. Along the north shore of Kachemak Bay, mammoth remains have been discovered on the beaches between Homer and the Anchor River.

Judy Winn was collecting coal near the base of the Homer Spit in 1976 when she noticed an unusual object. Ever curious, the Homer artist walked over to look. Among the rocks, seaweed and chunks of coal was a fragment of an old-looking tusk. Judy was surprised and perplexed. Could it be from a mammoth or a mastodon? And, how did it come to be on the Homer Spit? She felt strongly that it was an unusual discovery so she took the tusk home, pondered its existence in this place and shared her find with others.

Other mammoth parts have been discovered more recently. Two molars, an ankle bone and another tusk fragment were found by four people between 1991 and 2007. All were from the beaches between the Homer Spit and the mouth of the Anchor River. None were discovered *in situ* so until that happens, scientists cannot say with certainty that mammoths occupied the Peninsula. There are unconfirmed reports of mammoth parts found near Ninilchik and in Halibut Cove.

An astralagus, an ankle bone from the hind foot of a woolly mammoth, and this molar, which weighs slightly over three pounds, eroded from the sea bluffs of the north shore or were deposited by the currents and tides on area beaches.

Ankle bone. *Drawing by Lee Post*

Molar. *Drawing by Bill Kitzmiller*

Two tusk fragments, two molars and an ankle bone do not a mammoth make. How many animals do they actually represent? (Let's assume that there are two.) Do these enigmatic discoveries mean that woolly mammoths inhabited the Kenai Peninsula? Not necessarily. Contemporary literature indicates that mammoths did not occupy this region during the late Pleistocene because it was buried under dense glacial ice; however, current evidence suggests that mammoths might have occupied other regions of Alaska much more recently than previously thought.

If the great grazers did not inhabit the Peninsula, how do scientists explain their remains? Several scenarios come to mind. Could the animals have died, been trapped in glacial ice far from the Peninsula and then transported and deposited here—like glaciers transported and deposited huge boulders from distant mountains? Or, possibly a person collected the remains elsewhere in Alaska, brought them to the Peninsula and then later discarded them, maybe tossed them over a bank into a stream. Or, farfetched as it seems, could someone be perpetrating another Piltdown hoax, e.g. "planting" bones where they don't belong? The Piltdown puzzler involved the excavation of parts of a human skull and an apelike jawbone near Piltdown, England, between 1911 and 1915. Many archaeologists and scientists of that time believed that the discovery represented a significant new chapter in the story of human evolution. Decades later, the Piltdown bones were tested with modern dating methods. The ancient-looking jawbone had been deliberately aged and was actually from a modern chimpanzee. The hoax was revealed about 1953 yet the perpetrator was never found. While this latter scenario seems farfetched, the precedent was established with the Piltdown hoax. Regardless of how the mammoth parts got here, five were found on beaches and one in a river bed, suggesting that they washed down waterways such as Deep Creek and the Anchor River or eroded from the sea bluffs.

Wouldn't it be wonderful if mammoths did, indeed, occupy the Kenai Peninsula? Was there a window of time when the Peninsula was available to these creatures? At one time, the Caribou Hills were a refugium—an area where one or more species survived after the extinction of others in the adjacent environment. Could mammoths have found refuge there?

Mammoth. *Drawing by Kay VanDervoort*

17

Richard Reger of Soldotna, a retired geologist, has spent much of his career and now his retirement exploring the Peninsula. While he admits that our present knowledge precludes the presence of mammoths on the Kenai, he keeps an open mind and open eyes when he explores Kachemak Bay. To the author, open-mindedness is an important trait to nurture, especially in Alaska. Here, lay people can provide new information and help scientists learn about the dynamic environment. Hopefully, the next lucky person to find a mammoth treasure will contact a scientist or museum curator so that the discovery can be carefully and properly documented; however, if no other specimens are found, then the mammoth mystery will remain precisely that.

Toward the end of the Pleistocene Epoch another period of worldwide warming occurred, accompanied by the melting of glaciers. Between 16,000 to 10,000 years ago, the main features of Kachemak Bay, such as islands and embayments, were revealed. Raw bedrock was exposed as glaciers retreated. Over time, plants sprouted from wind-blown seeds and spores and slowly converted bedrock into soil. For centuries, coastal tundra dominated the region, but eventually it gave way to shrub birch, willow, alder and poplar, grasses and flowering plants. The dense spruce so characteristic of the north and south shores today would not arrive for many thousands of years.

Unique to the north shore are beds of burnt shale, burned when seams of coal spontaneously combusted under very specific natural conditions. Heat from the burning coal baked the adjacent shale into beds of an orangish or reddish chalk-like rock called chalkstone or baked shale. The late Frederica de Laguna, pioneer archaeologist in Kachemak Country, noted that the burning coal "gives off a most unpleasant stench . . ." Many residents like the idea that the word "Kachemak" is derived from a Native word meaning 'smoky bay.' Linguists, however, have been unable to confirm its meaning. In 1778 when Captain James Cook sailed into Shelikof Strait on the western shore of Cook Inlet, he named a large embayment *there* Smokey Bay.

FORMATION OF THE HOMER SPIT

The Homer Spit, photographed in November 1946, is the iconic image of the north shore. Its origins began with ancient snowflakes that fell in the distant Kenai Mountains and metamorphosed into glacial ice. *Helen Alm Collection*

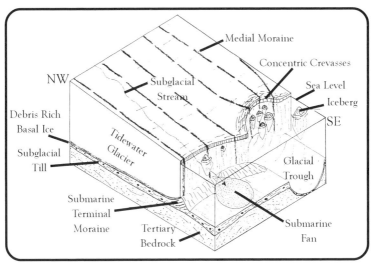

Believed to be a terminal moraine, the Spit formed about 15,000 to 14,000 years ago as glaciers reached their maximum forward movement then, with climate change, began to melt. As glacial ice melted, sand, gravels and rocks fell out and accumulated in one area, forming a moraine. Over time, coal and other materials were deposited atop the moraine by currents and, through accretion, land rose above sea level. *Courtesy of Richard Reger and the Pratt Museum*

The Homer Spit is ever-changing. Although naturally formed, today select areas are stabilized with huge boulders and a 30-acre staging area was constructed near the tip. Although once forested with spruce and carpeted with grasses and flowering plants, only remnant vegetation remains. A few shell middens, washed away in the 1990s, indicated the former use of the Spit by Native peoples; however, it was coal in the nearby bluffs that brought commercial development to the Spit in the 1880s.

Today, the lengthy, narrow and radically altered landmark is a patchwork of industrial, recreational, commercial and conservation land. The Homer Small Boat Harbor, one of the largest in the country, is homeport to a flotilla of recreational and commercial boats, several research vessels and, often, a U.S. Coast Guard vessel. It is a bustling harbor, especially in summer.

Homer is the largest community on the north shore. In 2008, an estimated 5,454 residents occupied the 25 square miles extending from the tip of the Spit across the bench and into the hills.

EARTH MOVERS

The majority of the world's volcanoes and earthquakes occur along a 25,000-mile-long horseshoe-shaped region arching from Washington northwestward along British Columbia, across southern and Southcentral Alaska, along the Aleutian Chain and then southwestward from Russia to Japan. Often called the Ring of Fire, this is one of the most geologically active regions on earth.

Deep offshore in the Gulf of Alaska, the Pacific tectonic plate slides under the North American plate. As the land masses grind past one another, earth movement occurs. Earthquakes can occur at any time and at any place in this dynamic environment. Numerous quakes have had their epicenter, or point of origin, near the mouth of Kachemak Bay, at Bradley Lake, in the Caribou Hills and in Homer itself. Earth movement can be caused also by volcanic eruptions and/or massive landslides.

The great Alaskan earthquake of 1964, whose epicenter was in Prince William Sound northeast of Kachemak Bay, caused considerable damage throughout Southcentral Alaska. (See chapter titled "Unsettling.")

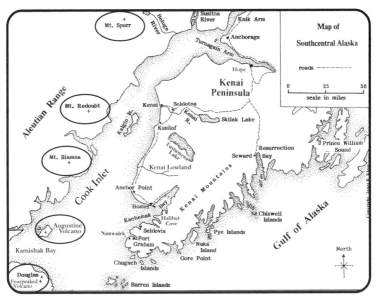

Strung like beads on the chain of the Aleutian Range are five volcanoes visible from Kachemak Bay: Fourpeaked, Douglas, Augustine, Iliamna and Redoubt. At the north end of the chain stands Mount Spurr in the Tordrillo Mountains. *Map by Victoria Hand; updated by Elaine Williamson*

No volcanoes exist in Kachemak Country; however, eruptive activity originating from those along the western shore of Cook Inlet has impacted and will continue to impact this region. Nearest Kachemak Bay is Augustine Volcano which rises in Kamishak Bay about 70 miles southwest of Homer. The volcano and the island it has formed, also called Augustine, are synonymous, each is the other. The Chigmit Mountains beyond Augustine are not visible from sea level so the classically shaped cone appears solitary and spectacular from viewpoints around Kachemak Bay.

The footprint of Augustine covers about 36 square miles which is subject to change with any eruption. At around 4,100 feet, Augustine seems short when compared to Mounts Iliamna and Redoubt, which soar to over 10,000 feet, and Mount Douglas and Fourpeaked Mountain, which rise almost 7,000 feet.

21

Those peaks, however, emerge from mountain ranges whereas Augustine rises directly from the sea. (Fourpeaked Mountain, which had been somnolent for thousands of years, began emitting steam and gas vapors in September 2006.)

Kachemak residents keep a close eye on Mount Augustine because of its unpredictable nature and its proximity to about half the population of Alaska, marine shipping lines, oil and gas facilities, the fisheries of Cook Inlet and the adjacent national park lands, refuge lands and critical habitat areas. *Game McGimsey and Alaska Volcano Observatory*

Augustine is the youngest, most frequently active, most unpredictable and potentially the most explosive of the neighboring volcanoes. It erupted into existence 19,000 to 15,500 years ago. Historical eruptions occurred in 1812, 1883, 1908, 1935, 1963 to 1964, 1976, 1986 and 2006. Some were minor and localized; others highly explosive with widespread effects. Typically, an eruption consists of phases of activity and quiescence spanning several months. Eruptions in 1986 and 2006 created mud and pyroclastic flows and blasted gray, feather-light ash over 30,000 feet into the air. When capricious winds disperse ash throughout Southcentral Alaska, air traffic may be disrupted or even grounded.

Evidence of eruptions occurring prior to 1812 is visible in ash layers in the stratigraphy of Kachemak Bay, and in ash deposits exposed on the flanks of Augustine itself.

The year 1883 was a year of intense volcanic activity. In Indonesia, Krakatoa erupted catastrophically in August and the resulting tsunami caused extensive death and destruction. Meteorological conditions were disturbed worldwide as dense ash, floating in the upper atmosphere, cast a chilling pall over the globe and lowered the world's temperature. Six weeks after Krakatoa blew, Augustine erupted. The event triggered a massive collapse of the north flank and about 25 minutes later a wave, reported to be 22 to 27-feet high, crashed onto the beaches of English Bay. According to descendants of the eyewitnesses, the October 6 tsunami arrived at low tide which saved the people and their settlement. A similar wave likely crashed onto and flooded over the Homer Spit.

"During the two hours which I spent in watching on the outer edge of the crater, it was estimated that not more than 30 consecutive seconds elapsed during which the masses of rock were not clattering down that portion of the inner core which was in sight from my station," wrote U.S. Geological Survey geologist George Becker in 1895. He and C. W. Purington were probably the first Americans to climb Augustine. *U.S. Geological Survey, 18th Annual Report. Original modified by Kay VanDervoort*

Although usually conical-shaped with a slightly flattened peak, shape-shifting of Augustine's profile can occur through a phantasmagorical phenomenon known as fata morgana. Named for Morgan le Fay, the mythical enchantress who played tricks on mariners, the complex mirage occurs when there are alternating layers of cold and warm air near the ground or the surface of water. A fata morgana can alter the classic silhouette of Augustine into an hourglass, a flat-topped butte, a castle in the air or any number of ethereal images.

Augustine has had many names. To the Alutiiq people it was known as *Utakineq*, simply meaning 'volcano,' while the Dena'ina of the Lake Iliamna region named it *Chu Nula* meaning 'beaver's sleep.' Seeing it on Saint Augustine's day in 1778 prompted Cook to call it Saint Augustine's Island. A year later, Spanish explorers Ignatio de Arteaga and Juan Francisco de la Bodega y Quadra named it *Pan de Azucar*, or 'Sugar Loaf,' and Russians called it *Chernoburoy* or a variation thereof, which translates as 'black-brown.'

The remote island volcano is a haven for seals, birds and other wildlife. In the 1950s the territorial government of Alaska paid bounty hunters to kill animals such as eagles, bears, coyotes and seals which preyed on salmon. Seasonal camps were established on Augustine by hunters who killed seals and collected their noses to document their harvest. About that same time, the Pumice Stone Company of Anchorage hired men to gather pumice to convert into cinder blocks. Bounty-hunting and pumice-mining were relatively short-lived economies on Augustine yet they provided pocket cash for Peninsula residents.

Activity on Augustine has been seismically monitored since 1970. Sensors on its flanks record daily rumblings. Since 1985, the data has been sent electronically to the Alaska Volcano Observatory offices in Fairbanks and Anchorage. Seismic stations in Homer and Seldovia and at Bradley Lake also record earth movements originating from Augustine. Usually, however, the lovely peak lies relatively still, serene and somnolent on the western horizon.

It was into this dynamic environment, created by tectonic drift and uplift and land subsidence, eroded by wind, water, tides and tsunamis, shaken by earthquakes and volcanic eruptions and occupied by a surprising diversity of plant and animal life that people set foot over eight millennia ago. They built their cultures upon the resources found in the mountains, waters and hills of the Kachemak triptych.

Timeline of Russian and European Events 1741 to 1867

The arrivals of expeditions from Russia and Europe into Cook Inlet foreshadowed extraordinary events that would bring irreversible changes to the Native peoples and physical environment of Kachemak Country.

1741—Navigators Vitus Bering and Aleksei Chirikov sailed from Kamchatka, Russia, across the North Pacific Ocean to a land which they identified as separate from Russia. Captain Chirikov, aboard the *St. Paul*, returned safely to Russia but Captain Bering, commanding the *St. Peter*, wrecked upon a remote island.

1741
1760 1750
1770
1790
1800
1830 1810

George Steller, a German naturalist, and many shipmates survived winter, built a boat the next spring and returned to Kamchatka. Their cargo included luxuriously silky sea otter pelts which found a ready market in China and stimulated the fur rush to Alaska. Within a few years, independent Russian trappers and traders (*promyshlenniki*) were hunting sea otters along the Aleutian Islands. Eventually, fur trading companies were established and expanded their hunting into Kenay (Kenai) Bay, as the Russians called Cook Inlet. (Almost a century before Bering's and Chirikov's voyages, Russian cossack leader Semen Dezhnev ascertained that Siberia and Alaska were separate lands when he sailed through the Bering Strait. His discovery, however, was eclipsed by the 1741 expeditions.)

1762 or **1763**—Arsenti Aminak, an elder living on Kodiak, recounted seeing Russian ships near that island when just a boy of nine or ten. "Before that time we had never seen a ship; we had intercourse with the Aglegnutes of Aliaska (Alaska) peninsula, with the Tnaianas (Dena'ina) of the Kenai peninsula, and with the Koloshes (Tlingit). . . but ships and white men we did not know at all." Aminak also recalled that a warrior visited the Russian ship and returned with glass beads.

This is a very early reference to trade occurring among Native cultures and to them possessing glass beads.

1778—Captain James Cook was the first British navigator to sail the inlet which was later named in his honor. He sailed along both shores, was contacted by Native people, took possession of the land for Great Britain and bestowed place names upon prominent features. Captain Cook lost an anchor from the *HMS Resolution* at a point not far from the mouth of a river. The point near which he lost the anchor became known as Anchor Point and is one of the oldest place names in Cook Inlet.

1785—*Sel'devaia Bukhta* (Seldovia) is mentioned in Russian documents as a Native village and temporary camp of Chugachmiuts (people from Chugach Bay, now Prince William Sound).

1786—A party of Russians and Native hunters camped near a lagoon at the mouth of Kachemak Bay. Later that summer, the

Shelikhov-Golikov Company established Alexandrovsk, a fur trading post, making it the first and oldest historic settlement on mainland Alaska. The river which ran past the post and then into Cook Inlet hosted salmon which provided food for the fur traders. (Alexandrovsk or Fort Alexander later became known as English Bay probably because it was mapped by British Captains Nathaniel Portlock and George Dixon that same summer. Today it is known as Nanwalek. The name used in this book is usually the one most appropriate to the time, e.g. during the Russian occupation it is referred to as Fort Alexander or Alexandrovsk, from 1867 to 1992 it is known as English Bay and after that it is called Nanwalek.)

As the pursuit and acquisition of sea otter furs intensified, Russian trading posts were established throughout Cook Inlet. Natives left their small, remote encampments to settle near the posts and, by doing so, changed the dynamics of their lives and livelihoods.

Sailing aboard the *King George* and the *Queen Charlotte*, respectively, Portlock and Dixon undertook a commercial fur trading expedition to Cook Inlet. They visited the Russians and Natives from Kodiak and Unalaska who resided at Fort Alexander. Portlock noted that the men subsisted primarily upon salmon and the root of the chocolate lily. (The plant is also known as Indian rice and Eskimo potato.) Upon surveying the area, the Englishmen found coal and named the area Coal Harbour (Harbor) and Graham Bay (today Port Graham waterway). Captain Dixon also described and illustrated a previously unknown shellfish, the razor clam.

North of Kachemak Bay, Russian fur traders built two log cabins within a stockade near the mouth of the Kasilof River and named it St. George.

1786-1867—The Russian period on the Kenai Peninsula was characterized by the introduction of the fur trade and trading posts, of manufactured tools, tobacco, intoxicating drinks and Russian clothing and food. The disintegration of the Dena'ina social organization occurred as did the death of uncounted Natives from intermittent warfare and diseases, especially smallpox in 1838 to 1840. Russians documented the natural resources, charted the coastline, recorded Native words and collected innumerable cultural objects which remain preserved in museums. Priests introduced the Russian Orthodox religion, established churches in Alexandrovsk and Seldovia and preserved some Native traditions.

1788–Navigator Gerasim Ismailof claimed Cook Inlet for Russia when he and the cossack Bocharov buried a possession plate near Alexandrovsk. Although sought by many people, the location of the rare artifact remains unknown.

Records report the establishment of a large Russian *artel* (a settlement, often fortified) of *promyshlenniki* in the vicinity of *Tonkii Mys*, *Kachemakskaia* (Homer Spit, Kachemak Bay). Supposedly 20 fur traders built their *artel* near a settlement of Kenaitze (Dena'ina). While no physical proof of the *artel* has been found, contemporary authors Solovjova and Vovnyanko suggest that the area known today as Kachemak City is a "most plausible place" for its location.

1790–In July, Spanish navigator Salvador Fidalgo visited Alexandrovsk. He described the Russian enclave as consisting of a square wooden house with a central courtyard, a sentry box with a guard, a blacksmith's shop, kitchen, barracks, storerooms in which the residents kept whale blubber, dried fish and fishing gear, and a room with two very large caldrons in which to store whale oil. Twenty-one Russians, including six guards, protected the fort with swivel guns. Each man had a musket, pistol and saber. Several huts of "Indians" lived nearby. Fidalgo noted that the Russians and "Indians" spent their summers fishing and hunting birds and animals such as sea otters, sea lions, bears, foxes and other furbearers.

The Spanish explorer claimed the land for Spain and buried a bottle containing documents of possession. He also sailed into Port Graham waterway which he named Puerto de Revillagigedo (Harbor of Revillagigedo). Like others, Fidalgo sailed past Kachemak Bay which he acknowledged as a "great bay of much depth and without any shelter."

When navigators such as Fidalgo, Cook, Portlock, Dixon and Vancouver bypassed Kachemak Bay, they must have been able to tell by the lay of the land that it was not a major waterway. Also, having no obvious shelter would have discouraged sailors from exploring it.

1791—Russian fur traders built Fort St. Nicholas, a trading post, near the mouth of the Kenai River.

1791-1797—During these tumultuous years, intense competition for furs and trading rights in Cook Inlet caused warfare between the Lebedev-Lastochkin Company and the Shelikhov Company. Skirmishes also occurred among the Russians and Native peoples, including the Dena'ina and Alutiit in Southcentral Alaska. The violence ended in 1797 when the Kenaitze Dena'ina ousted the Lebedev-Lastochkin Company.

1793—The Lebedev-Lastochkin Company established a post on Kachemak Bay in an attempt to oust the Shelikhov Company which had established a winter camp near the entrance to Cook Inlet. The winter camp was Alexandrovsk. The location of the post on Kachemak Bay remains unknown.

1794—British Captain George Vancouver, who had sailed with Captain Cook, reexplored much of Cook Inlet.

Although documentation is scarce, local lore states that Russians from Fort St. Nicholas (Kenai) abducted women and children from the Native settlement of Soonroodna in Kachemak Bay.

1796-1799—The Russian American Company was established and granted full trading privileges from the Tsar along the coast of Alaska for the next two decades, effectively eliminating the Lebedev-Lastochkin and the Shelikhov companies.

1844—Former employees of the Russian American Company and their families established the agricultural settlements of Kachemak, Kasilof, Kenai and Ninilchik in the Cook Inlet region. The location of Kachemak remains unknown; however, the north shore seems like the best location for an agricultural colony.

1848-1850—Peter Doroshin, a mining engineer, investigated the mineral resources of the Kenai Peninsula and reported coal near Alexandrovsk. He probably located the same outcrop that Portlock and Dixon had noted about six decades earlier.

1849—Cook Inlet was charted by a Russian survey party headed by Captain Archimandritof for whom the shoals, west of the Homer Spit, were named.

1852—Mikhail Tebenkov, governor of Russian America from 1845 to 1850, published the *Atlas of the Northwest Coasts of America.* Chart V depicts Kachemak Bay with numerous Russian place names.

1855 to about **1865**—The Russian American Company mined coal at Coal Village on Port Graham. The village contained over 20 dwellings making it the third largest European settlement in the Russian colonies.

1867—The Russian period ended with the sale of Alaska to the United States. During the 126 years of Russian control, more than 225 expeditions mapped, charted and explored the North Pacific including much of coastal Alaska. Artists, biologists, botanists, ethnographers, geologists and others described and collected countless specimens and documented the life ways and material culture of Native Alaskans.

Place names across Alaska acknowledge the men, of many nationalities, who sailed on those expeditions, including Bering, Chamisso, Eschscholtz, Kotzebue, Krusenstern, Steller and Voznesenski (Wosnesenski), for whom a glacier was named in Kachemak Bay. Although Russian exploration essentially ended with the sale of Alaska, Orthodox priests continued to establish and practice their religion in the communities along the shores of Kachemak Bay.

The firm of Hutchinson, Kohl, and Company acquired some assets of the Russian American Company. In 1872, the three-year-old Alaska Commercial Company purchased the property of Hutchinson, Kohl, and Company and assumed ownership and management of trading posts throughout much of the new American territory.

CHANGING TIMES, CHANGING CULTURES

Kachemak Country in the 1800s was a crossroads for cultures as it had been for millennia. The ancestral Natives had moved here from many regions of Alaska such as the Alaska Peninsula, Bristol Bay and the Kodiak archipelago. More recently, Alutiiq people from Prince William Sound and Dena'ina, from interior Alaska, had migrated here. Radiocarbon dates from Halibut Cove indicate that Dena'ina were living there around A.D. 1200.

In the first half of the nineteenth century, Natives in Kachemak Country retained a fairly traditional life of hunting,

fishing and gathering, traveling in kayaks and living in small groups at Anchor Point and Bear Cove, on the islands in Eldred Passage, and in Seldovia and Fort Alexander. But irreversible changes had occurred, changes which meant the loss and replacement of traditional beliefs, materials, and technologies with ones introduced by newcomers from afar.

Natives harvest salmon from artificially built ponds on a beach in Kachemak Bay. *Oil painting on wood by Louis Nagy, Sr. Courtesy of Seldovia Native Association, Inc.*

A major catalyst of change was the arrival of Russian fur traders and the opening of trading posts. Russians built the first trading post on mainland Alaska at Alexandrovsk about 1786. With the opening of other posts around Cook Inlet, many Natives deserted their small settlements, moved nearer to the posts and inadvertently created new communities and accelerated change. After the purchase of Alaska, the Alaska Commercial Company (ACC) operated the trading post at Alexandrovsk, then becoming known as English Bay. In Seldovia, ACC and the Western Fur Trading Company maintained posts while in Anchor Point, the Granroos family managed a private trading business in their home in the early 1900s.

Initially, Natives traded pelts of luxuriously furred marine and land animals for Russian and European goods such as axes, pots and pans, guns, glass beads and glassware. Increasingly, American-made goods replaced foreign wares and eventually money replaced barter.

The Kenai Peninsula was rich in animal life. Henry Wood Elliott, a naturalist and artist who visited Alaska repeatedly in the 1800s, wrote that,

"The greatest number of different mammals found wild in any one region of Alaska is to be recorded here: bears, brown and black; deer (moose), reindeer (caribou) and the woodland caribou; big-horn mountain sheep (Dall sheep), a long-haired variety (mountain goat). These animals are all shot. The trapped varieties are: beaver, land-otter, porcupines, whistling marmot or woodchuck, large grey wolves, lynx, wolverine, marten, mink, ermine, weasels, and muskrats."

Marmot. *Drawing by Lee Post*

Residents and visitors had access to prime hunting and trapping grounds, one reason for the existence of trading posts and for the influx of big-game hunters at the end of the 1800s and into the 1900s.

In Kachemak Bay, Natives were attracted to Yukon Island. The Dena'ina called it *Nika'a*, meaning 'big island,' and the Alutiit called it *Nikraq*, no translation. Abrupt rock cliffs characterize the east, north and west shores while level ground fronted by accessible beaches defines the southeast and southwest shores. Springs supplied fresh water, tide pools provided habitat for edible invertebrates and deep adjacent waters were frequented by seabirds, seals, otters, sea lions and whales.

33

A computer map shows a section of the south shore. Yukon is the large island in the upper center. The three embayments cutting into the south shore are, from left, Jakolof Bay, Tutka Bay and Sadie Cove. *Steve Baird, Kachemak Bay Research Reserve. Based on data from U.S. Geological Survey*

When W. H. Dall and Marcus Baker charted much of the coast of Alaska for the U.S. Coast and Geodetic Survey, they sailed aboard the 84-foot-long Gloucester model schooner, *Yukon*. In 1880, Dall bestowed the schooner's name upon the island in Kachemak Bay. *Courtesy of NOAA Photo Library, Central Library; Office of NOAA Corps Operations*

Much of what is known about the residents of Yukon Island has been learned through archaeology, the scientific excavation of a site and the subsequent analysis of recovered information and objects. Materials from excavations indicate that Eskimo, Dena'ina, Russians and Americans occupied the island. As of 2008, the earliest known residents settled there over three millennia ago.

A search for the geographic and cultural origin of decorated stone lamps, such as this, compelled Frederica de Laguna to visit Southcentral Alaska from the University of Pennsylvania, during the summers of 1930 to 1932. *The University Museum, Neg. # S8-12354, University of Pennsylvania*

De Laguna's deepest and most extensive excavation occurred on the southwest-facing beach on Yukon Island where she and her crew found abundant materials related to an ancient culture of Eskimo marine mammal hunters and fishermen. When her field crew had begun the excavation, they had dug through a four-to ten-foot high bank full of glass bottles and beads, metal objects, invertebrate shells and animal bones. That bank had eroded to ground level by the mid-1990s. Due to tidal erosion, uncounted objects had washed away. The objects considered modern by de Laguna were considered historic 60 years later. To save what remained of the site, Peter Zollars, archaeologist from Anchorage, and the author conducted a salvage dig with permission from the land manager, the U.S. Fish and Wildlife Service. During the summer of 1996, many dedicated volunteers dug, catalogued artifacts and participated in camp chores.

Frederica de Laguna holds a stray cat which found a temporary home with the archaeologists on Yukon Island in 1932. *Courtesy of Bill Newman*

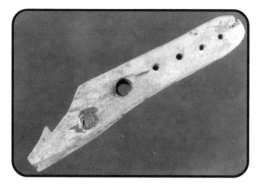

This toggling harpoon head strongly suggests an ancient Eskimo-style tool yet the metal rivets make it a classic transitional object.

By the end of the field season, a trench about fifteen-feet-long, nine-feet-wide and three-and-one-half-feet-deep had been excavated. One thousand fifty-six artifacts were logged into the catalog. Few were intact. Even though broken, cut, dirty and worn, they told of life in Kachemak Bay in the mid-to-second half of the 1800s. To differentiate the site from others nearby, it was designated SEL 001, Historic Midden, by the Office of History and Archaeology, State of Alaska.

Who occupied the sheltered cove over a century ago? "In historic times it was territory contested by local Eskimo and Tanaina (Dena'ina) Indians," wrote de Laguna in 1998 in a letter to John Martin, manager, U.S. Fish and Wildlife Service. According to the late elder Peter Kalifornsky, the island was a Dena'ina village until late into the 1800s. While most artifacts appeared to be associated with a Dena'ina occupation, some exhibited Eskimo traits.

Wassila, born on Yukon Island about 1870, exemplified the ethnicity of many Native peoples living in Southcentral Alaska. He was half Kodiak Eskimo on his father's side, a quarter Russian through his mother's lineage and grew up in the Dena'ina culture. (Cornelius Osgood, the ethnographer, did not mention whether or not Wassila grew up on Yukon Island; however, the tools he and his people used may have reflected his mixed heritage.)

At some unknown point in time and for reasons unknown, the settlement was abandoned. When W. H. Dall named Yukon Island in 1880 and J.A. Jacobsen visited it in 1883, neither mentioned a village. What happened to the residents? No one knows. Archaeologists can only surmise that they moved elsewhere and, when doing so, left behind a wonderfully eclectic collection of objects.

THE HISTORIC MIDDEN

Household goods were plentiful. Metal spoons, forks and knives were scattered among fragments of drinking glasses and serving dishes while a porcelain flower vase rested alongside a whale vertebra. Pieces of thick terra cotta crocks contrasted with sherds of delicate British-made tea cups, saucers, plates and bowls. Occasionally tiny, precisely drilled holes were noticed in sherds suggesting that they had been tied together, possibly to prolong the usefulness of the dish.

Teacups and saucers were precious objects, even status symbols among Dena'ina hunters, according to Anchorage archaeologist Karen Wood Workman. In 1980 and 1981 she excavated what she and her husband, William Workman, now Professor Emeritus, Department of Anthropology, University of Alaska Anchorage, identified as an historic Dena'ina site on Chugachik Island. It contained many cup and saucer sherds. So, it was no surprise to excavate hundreds of sherds on Yukon Island. At least 35 patterns such as British Flowers and Filigree, were identified. Most were manufactured at the Spode Pottery, in central England. Spode had an exclusive trade agreement with the Hudson Bay Company to provide earthenware to its posts from 1836 to 1853. The HBC post at Fort Vancouver, Washington, exported British-manufactured items to trading outlets in Alaska.

A door knob, a brick and slivers of window glass spoke of former structures. Occasionally, the compact dirt of a house floor was identified but missing were floor boards, wall boards and roof elements. Their absence suggested that the structures had been dismantled and removed or that they had deteriorated and been obliterated by time and, possibly, tides.

Pottery sherds.
Drawings by
Kay VanDervoort

37

A rusted padlock from a traveling trunk was unearthed but it was a miniature trunk that caught Henry Wood Elliott's attention. While in Cook Inlet in 1886, he visited a Kenaitze Dena'ina home and wrote:

"No furniture annoys the Kenai housekeeper, unless the small square blocks of wood used occasionally as stools or seats can be so styled; the grease and fire-boxes which we have seen in Sitkan households are also duplicated here, but though made of wood they are not so neatly put together. The traders recently have introduced a very novel feature to the interior of nearly every Kenaitze house: it is the common, cheap, box-imitation, *in miniature*, of a Saratoga trunk with lock and key. Those oddly contrasted articles will be found everywhere among these people, who keep in them all their valuables, such as charms, and toys for the children, flashy handkerchiefs, small tools fashioned out of bits of iron and steel, bags of thread and stripped sinews, needles, ammunition, and their percussion-caps, which are to them as pearls without price–nothing so precious. They crave nothing from the white trader save powder, lead, good rifles, percussion-caps, tobacco, calico, and the sham trunks alluded to." Percussion caps. *Drawings by Lee Post*

Personal items uncovered during the excavation, included footware, fabric, sewing thimbles, glass trade beads and even commercially manufactured paint. Pieces of leather from boots and shoes were fairly common in the midden. All the boot leather had been cut and most of the metal grommets and hob nails removed, possibly to convert into more desirable items. Most remnants of footware were clustered in one place—a cobbler's work area?

Several wads of frieze, a thick, black-green fabric, were excavated.

The woolen cloth, also called soldier's cloth, served as coat material for people of the lower class in Russia. In 1794 British Captain Vancouver noted that many Natives wore frieze jackets while the Russians preferred Native clothing. In Kenai Bay (Cook Inlet) Russians were content "to live after the manner of the native Indians... adopting the same fashion, and using the same materials for their apparel, and differing from them in their exterior appearance only by the want of paint on their faces..." Although buttons of bone, glass, metal and shell were unearthed, none were attached to the fabric.

Three metal sewing thimbles had tiny holes punched near their tops. Possibly a small stone or bead had hung inside each to make a tinkler or bell. The words "Forget-Me-Not" circled the rim of one thimble—a charming discovery as that is Alaska's state flower.

Common were pieces of white, ball clay smoking pipes with small bowls and long, thin stems. The letters, "T D," imprinted on several, suggested that they were manufactured by Thomas Dormer of England. During and after the American Civil War, Scottish and American manufacturers produced similar pipes so maybe not all were imported from England.

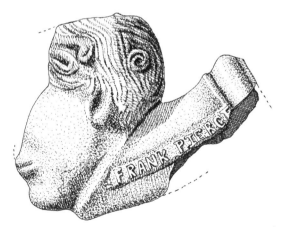

A rare find was the fragment of a red terra cotta presidential pipe crafted for Franklin Pierce, United States president from 1853 to 1857. Such pipes were advertising gimmicks to help a candidate campaign for the presidency or to celebrate his victory. *Drawing by Lee Post*

Glass trade beads were found throughout the excavation. One digger found a shell full of the tiny treasures. Cornaline d'Aleppo, round red beads with white hearts, and faceted "Russian" blues were favorites. These beads probably had decorated clothing and dangled from the ears, lips and noses of Native women and men. At one time, a single bead represented great wealth among Native people.

Unusual finds stimulated research. An elegant, dime-sized, round metal bead may have hung from a Russian Orthodox priest's vestment while small smears and lumps of a reddish clayey substance found in cockle shells appeared to be vermilion. This bright red cake paint, probably manufactured in China or France, supplemented or replaced the pigment traditionally made from red ocher or hematite. Paint would have decorated faces, tools, clothing and other objects.

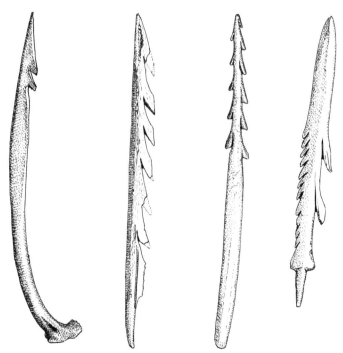

Bone hunting points were multi-barbed and fascinating in their uniqueness. The one on the left illustrates how a barbed point was carved from a marine mammal rib. *Drawings by Lee Post*

Hunting and fishing tools, found throughout the midden, included traditional stone implements such as a hone, numerous hammerstones, pumice and baked shale abraders and boulder spalls—those multi-functional chips of stone found in sites throughout Kachemak Bay. Aboriginal tools crafted from bone included fishing hooks, a toggling harpoon head and sea otter points, among others. Territorial law required that Native hunters use traditional tools to kill sea otters so the small bone points were still crafted at this time. Alongside the time-honored tools were ones crafted of metal.

Sea otter points.
Drawings by Kay VanDervoort

A grayish beluga whale calf swims alongside its white parent. Beluga bones were found throughout the site.
Drawing by Gary Lyon

Metal was highly desired by the Natives. They cut pieces from cast iron pots and shaped them into barbed points and they bent nails and spikes into J-shapes, possibly for fishing. Scraps of lead were heated and molded into musket balls. An awl and a small unidentified tool were crafted from copper possibly acquired from the Copper River Ahtna. Russian and American axe heads replaced indigenous hammerstones.

Armaments were extremely important and, fairly quickly, mass-produced rifles and pistols replaced aboriginal hunting tools. Excavated were flintlock rifle parts, gun flints, Henry .44 rimfire and Winchester center-fire shell casings, percussion caps and lids from gunpowder cans manufactured by the Hazard Powder Company of Connecticut.

41

American military insignia.
Drawings by Lee Post

A most unexpected discovery was that of pressed tin military insignia. Three spread-eagle pins, one numeral "2" and five crossed-canons were excavated. (Several more were accidentally discarded and rediscovered in the back dirt, the dirt that gets troweled then tossed aside by excavators.) Interestingly, the attachment pin on each was missing. The insignia probably date to the American Civil War of 1862 to 1865 and may have been worn in a vertical row on an officer's cap.

How did the insignia get to Yukon Island? After the Civil War ended, numerous military batteries were sent to the West Coast. Two years later, Alaska was purchased from Russia and the U.S. Army assumed command of the new territory. Battery F of the Second Artillery, stationed at Fort Vancouver, Washington, was reassigned to Alaska to establish a military presence in Cook Inlet. In July 1868, Lt. John McGilvray, commander, ordered the captain of the bark *Torrent* to sail into the Gulf of Chugachnik (Kachemak Bay) to establish a post to be called Fort Kenai. With the assistance of several Natives, McGilvray explored the (Homer) Spit and the adjacent benchland and found them lacking the basic amenities needed to erect and maintain a fort.

Upon completing his exploration, McGilvray directed the ship's captain to sail toward the entrance to Cook Inlet to explore other locations. On July 15, near the entrance to Port Graham, the *Torrent* ran aground upon a reef. (In July 2008, a cannon and cannon balls, portholes, a metal toilet bowl and other objects were recovered by representatives from the State of Alaska, the federal government and private citizens.)

Lifeboats make for shore after the *Torrent* ran aground. A survivor sketched this image as the configuration of the distinctively shaped rocks is quite accurate. *B79.87.3, Anchorage Museum*

All passengers associated with Battery F and the full crew of sailors survived. Salvaged were three mountain Howitzers, about 50 muskets, 48 revolvers, five mules, two flat-boats, a life boat, a small boat, a few gun-carriages, wagon wheels and a 30-day supply of flour and pork. Using smaller boats, survivors revisited the *Torrent* to salvage whatever they could. The military insignia could have been recovered from the wreck, come ashore on the clothing of the soldiers or simply washed ashore later.

The shipwrecked passengers bivouacked near the former Russian trading post of Alexandrovsk. Still standing were a few unoccupied log huts and the ruins of an old church with its cracked bell. In a river nearby, the survivors found abundant salmon.

Several weeks after the shipwreck, the steamer *Fideliter* arrived and transported the survivors to Kodiak Island. After wintering there, Battery F finally established Fort Kenai about 70 miles north of Kachemak Bay. While stationed there, soldiers could have sold, given away or traded the insignia or the thin tin emblems could have entered the trade system when soldiers retired, deserted and/or married local women. Due to the lack of Native uprisings, the fort was decommissioned in 1870 and Battery F returned to the Presidio of San Francisco for reassignment.

Three men visit the ruins of the old blacksmith of the Russian colony at English Bay in this undated postcard. *Courtesy of Resurrection Bay Historical Society, Seward*

The insignia, the Franklin Pierce pipe and the Hazard Powder cans help date the Historic Midden to the mid-to-late 1800s.

Artifacts reveal only so much about a culture. While an abundance of bone, stone, metal, glass and earthenware objects was excavated, missing were objects crafted from organic materials such as wood, nettles, birch bark and grass. No objects sewn from mammal, bird or fish skins were unearthed. Such items were probably taken when the people left Yukon Island and any remaining probably deteriorated and/or washed away with the passage of time.

The Yukon Islanders enjoyed a great variety of foods as indicated by the profusion of bones and shells which Lee Post, a scientific illustrator and bone identification specialist, analyzed.

Cornelius Osgood listed 47 species of animals of economic value to the Dena'ina of Cook Inlet. Fish, marine mammals and invertebrates constitute half of the species on his list. Most occupy the waters of Kachemak Bay for at least part of the year. From the land the Dena'ina harvested marmot, porcupine, wolverine, marten, fox and bear. From chill waters they pulled porpoise, seals, sea otters, beluga and fish. Cormorants, ducks, gulls, loons, murres, shearwaters and at least one albatross were harvested also.

The albatross bone was particularly interesting. While investigating the fisheries of Alaska in 1880, Tarleton Bean visited English Bay and wrote, "We found it (short-tailed albatross) at various points. . . but the mouth of Cook's Inlet, and the vicinity of the Barren Islands, seemed to be its favorite summer resort. Natives of the trading village Alexandrovsk frequently spear this bird from their bidarkas (boats). I picked up four skins of this species from a pile of refuse at this village." (Within several decades of Bean's visit, short-tailed albatross numbers had declined rapidly. Although the species is close to extinction, it has rebounded slightly.)

David Yesner, Professor of Anthropology at the University of Alaska Anchorage, told the author that a healthy percentage of the bird bones in ancient sites in Kachemak Bay were from albatross. When the last of the long-winged, low-flying short-tailed albatross soared over Kachemak Bay is uncertain but just to know that they were living in this environment not too long ago is fascinating.

Puffins, such as the tufted puffin, left, and the horned puffin, provided not only meat, bones, and feathers and skin for clothing but beaks to dangle and clack on Dena'ina dance rattles. *Drawings by Kay VanDervoort*

Yukon Islanders also harvested clams, mussels, whelks and other invertebrates from nearby shoals and tide pools. Discarded shells comprised the bulk of the Historic Midden. Although inedible, a sand dollar fragment was unearthed, strongly suggesting that these echinoderms have inhabited local beaches since at least the 1800s. Gretchen Abbott Bersch and Zach Porter recall sand dollars living in the substrate near their childhood homes on Yukon Island and Sunshine Point, respectively. Although none have been reported from Yukon in recent years, a bed persists near Sunshine Point and also on MacDonald Spit.

Plants deteriorate quickly in the acidic soils of Kachemak Bay so it was a pleasant surprise to unearth several piles of seeds from elder bushes. Did the inhabitants cook and extract the juice from elder berries as contemporary residents do?

Natives from Nanwalek, Port Graham and Seldovia have ancestral ties to Yukon Island. The big island offered the many amenities needed to develop permanent communities. The lure of Yukon remains evident and enduring—people have lived along its shores for the past 3,500 years.

Henry Wood Elliott painted the watercolor, Natives Hunting the White Whale, Cook's Inlet, Alaska, in 1883 after visiting the Kenai Peninsula. Steam rises from Mt. Iliamna in the background. *NOAA National Marine Fisheries Service*

UNRAVELING THE SECRETS OF SOONROODNA

At the end of the nineteenth century museum personnel, particularly in the United States and Europe, believed that aboriginal cultures throughout the world were becoming extinct. To assure that knowledge of them would not be lost, museums sent collectors around the globe to obtain information and objects representing such cultures. Numerous collectors visited Alaska. Among them was Johan Adrian Jacobsen, an intrepid Norwegian who was collecting for the Royal Ethnological Museum in Berlin, Germany, (later named the Museum für Völkerkunde, today the Ethnologisches Museum Berlin).

During his travels along the Pacific Northwest Coast and in Alaska from 1881 to 1883, Jacobsen amassed 6,720 objects representing the oldest, most traditional objects he could find.

Jacobsen, photographed shortly before his trip to the Pacific Northwest and Alaska, was a passionate collector who visited Cook Inlet communities in 1883. *Ethnologisches Museum Berlin*

THE COOK INLET COLLECTION

Jacobsen was concluding his collecting journey when he trekked across the Alaska Peninsula to Iliamna Bay then sailed northward to the Dena'ina village of Tyonek. There he purchased about 59 items at the Alaska Commercial Company trading post. He then sailed across Cook Inlet to Fort Kenai where he acquired 24 more objects. After several days there, he boated southward, stopped briefly at Kasilof and Anchor Point then crossed Kachemak Bay to English Bay/Fort Alexander. From there he visited and collected about 65 objects from a long-abandoned Native settlement called Soonroodna.

Upon returning to Berlin, the collector spent two years cataloging the extensive Alaska collection. His original handwritten catalog cards, along with the majority of the objects, remain well organized and carefully curated. (The number of objects has varied over the years as some were confiscated, lost, misplaced and rediscovered during and after World War II.)

Eventually, Jacobsen wrote an account of his travels; however,

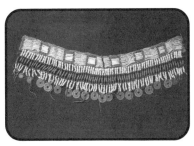

Jacobsen acquired this woman's belt decorated with dentalia, glass beads and Chinese coins and this leather hunting bag in Tyonek. At Fort Kenai, he obtained a woven grass hat adorned with wool and feathers, and four wooden elements (three shown in their entirety) of a porcupine snare. *Photograph of belt and hunting bag by Dietrich Graf, 1998; others by Martin Franken, 2005. Ethnologisches Museum Berlin*

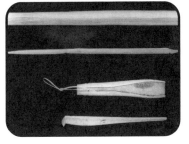

the book was ghost written for the public by Adrian Woldt, a German author. To enliven the book, Woldt exaggerated, downplayed, falsified or simply omitted information which compromised Jacobsen's account. Woldt even changed the original name of the village—from Sanradna as Jacobsen recorded it—to Soonroodna. Thus, all the information about Soonroodna needs to be questioned and analyzed.

In 1977, Erna Gunther translated the German text into English. From a mere three pages in *Alaskan Voyage 1881-1883, An Expedition to the Northwest Coast of America*, the tragedy of Soonroodna emerges.

The Soonroodna Story

Deep within Kachemak Country is hidden the lost village of Soonroodna. Although in the late 1700s Cook Inlet had been visited by numerous European explorers, by 1787 Russians had taken possession of the inlet. Two Russian fur trading companies claimed Cook Inlet and fought between themselves for the right to hunt sea otters. By the mid-1790s, they had almost exterminated the furry marine mammals. During those years, conflicts also occurred frequently between the Russians and the Dena'ina who occupied the shores of much of the inlet.

The residents of Kachemak Country did not escape the violence. Russians from Fort St. Nicholas (Fort Kenai) allegedly attacked Soonroodna in 1794 and abducted the women and children. The survivors abandoned the ravaged village, leaving behind many cultural objects. Intrigued by the story, Jacobsen hired Native men in English Bay and at Akedaknak in Seldovia Bay to take him to Soonroodna. They sailed to Yukon Island where they spent the night in a house that belonged to their Indian guide. The next morning, after several hours of sailing, the party arrived at the deserted settlement. Over the next three days Jacobsen collected about 65 objects from burial caves and from several excavations. Upon completing his excavations, he boated back to English Bay, sailed to Kodiak and then the West Coast, crossed the United States and returned to Berlin.

The Collection

In 2002 the author had the extraordinary opportunity to study the Soonroodna collection at the Ethnologisches Museum. Because her time was limited to a mere five days, she asked Peter Bolz, Curator of North American Ethnology, to show her what he believed to be the most unusual objects. Each was unique.

These are the only known masks believed to be from Kachemak Bay. Perforations along the outer edges were probably pegged with feathers or other ornamentation. Remnants of white, black and red paint remain visible on each. Likely carved from spruce, each is slowly deteriorating.

The three masks from Soonroodna were crafted in the distinctive style of the Chugach Alutiiq people from Prince William Sound. Each exhibits a wide forehead, a large nose and small eyes. One mask is strikingly similar to a dance mask collected in Prince William Sound before 1881. The nose of another appears to have been retouched with vermilion, a manufactured paint Natives acquired from Russian or American trading posts.

Jacobsen wrote that the old dance masks served as burial gifts and were stored in a cave where they remained as objects of "pious awe" for the descendants. People visiting the abandoned village left gifts to the masks which were viewed as spirits of the deceased. *Top and bottom photographs by Martin Franken, 2005. Middle photograph by Dietrich Graf, 1995. Ethnologisches Museum Berlin*

Although the masks appear to be of Alutiiq origin, other objects represent a Dena'ina origin. In 1930, Cornelius Osgood gathered information about the traditional Dena'ina culture during his work in Seldovia. He wrote that the Kachemak Bay Natives constructed a baby cradle using a bentwood rim, a sealskin covering and a moss stuffing and that it was inherited by one child after another. In the Soonroodna collection is a baby's cradle which fits that description.

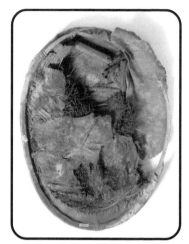

Baby cradle, 1883.
Photograph by Dietrich Graf, 1995.
Ethnologisches Museum Berlin

Another object is a wooden staff, about two inches in diameter and 28 inches tall. The vertical grooves, carved from the top to the bottom, are interrupted by four neatly incised horizontal rings. Small pieces of wood are spaced around each ring. Under one are fine strands of fiber. Osgood's description of a Dena'ina "devil stick" matches that of the Soonroodna staff except in length. The Soonroodna staff is shorter.

Aboriginal pottery is rare in Kachemak Bay yet Jacobsen excavated seven fragments, allegedly from two depths. Six had a fine matrix, were relatively thin, skillfully crafted and black from the smooth interior through to the smooth exterior. The seventh sherd was quite different; it was very thick, coarse, relatively light-colored and tempered with tiny round and angular black pebbles and white pebbles.

The objects from Soonroodna are of varied materials. Of the 65, almost half are of bone, a dozen of stone, nine of wood, seven of pottery, one of copper, one of skin and plant material, three of iron and two of glass. In *Alaskan Voyage. . .* it states that one glass bead was collected; actually, there are two, one light and one dark blue and of different shapes. A small collection of fauna included a broken sea otter skull, fish bones, one mammal tooth and a shell.

Carved from dense wood, this 15 inch-tall figure of a woman remains intact even though her nose is pierced and one ear has multiple holes along its length. Faint traces of red paint are evident under her nose and black paint on her cheeks, forehead and the back of her head. A well-defined groove around her hairline may have held an attachment. The rough scrapes on her chin suggest tattoo marks. *Photograph by Martin Franken, 2005. Ethnologisches Museum Berlin*

AGE OF THE SITE

How old is Soonroodna? Osgood states that, "There is little doubt that the site is historic, that it was deserted by its occupants, the Kachemak Bay Tanaina (Dena'ina), after the raiding party of the Russians . . ." He further states that the iron knives and glass bead (beads) were historic Russian trade objects. William Workman concurs that the upper component was historic and suggests that the deeper, older component, as represented by the pottery and bone and stone tools, represents a prehistoric occupation—that it dates to the time before the arrival of the Russians. The actual age of the village remains unknown but it was certainly occupied in the 1700s and probably considerably earlier.

THE LOCATION

One of the more enigmatic mysteries surrounding Soonroodna is its location. Where was it located? The Little Ice Age (LIA) provides a clue to its location. The LIA lasted from around A.D. 1300-1850 or even to 1900 as some scholars suggest. During this worldwide cooling period, many glaciers in Kachemak Bay were closer to tidewater.

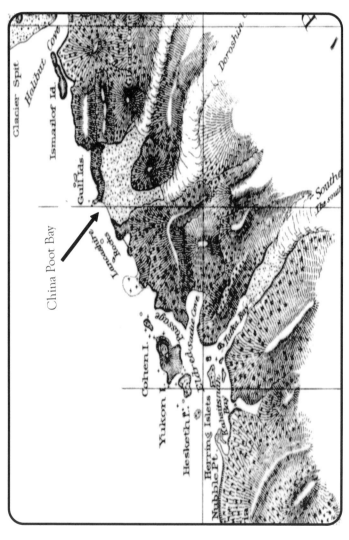

China Poot Bay

In 1895, China Poot Bay appeared as a glacial outwash plain. *U.S. Geological Survey, 17ᵗʰ Annual Report, Part I, Plate LI*

Jacobsen wrote that Soonroodna was ". . . situated at the foot of the third glacier on the south shore of Kachemak Bay." As he sailed through Eldred Passage and eastward in 1883, he could have seen the Southern, the Doroshin and, just beyond it, the Wosnesenski Glaciers. Based on their location at the end of the Little Ice Age, the author interprets the location of Soonroodna to be in China Poot Bay. Both Frederica de Laguna and the late historian Morgan Sherwood had reached the same conclusion years earlier. Sherwood wrote in a letter to the author in 1994, "You will see from Dall's map that the foot of the third glacier is China Poot."

Further evidence supporting the location of Soonroodna in China Poot Bay comes from the pottery Jacobsen unearthed. To date, potsherds have been excavated only at Soonroodna and on Yukon Island. De Laguna wrote that, "The Indian village site at Waterbury's place (a former fox farm), on the north side of the bay (China Poot), just inside the entrance, is supposed to be the oldest site in the region, according to the Indian tradition." A Port Graham Eskimo reported the village name to be *Tsa'yerqat* meaning 'cave,' because of the big caves just north of the entrance to China Poot Bay. De Laguna noted that one was supposed to have been a burial cave. Since 1964 when the area subsided, the caves of China Poot have been regularly flooded by high tides. Tidal erosion may have washed out the potsherds that Michael McBride, a resident of China Poot Bay, found at the fox farm years ago.

Several Dena'ina names have been suggested for Soonroodna. James Kari, a linguist with the Alaska Native Language Center in Fairbanks, listed the Dena'ina name as *Ts'enghutnu?* which is translated as 'bone fur stream?'. Dena'ina elder Peter Kalifornsky suggested the name *Chunghutnu?* and indicated it as a vaguely known site possibly in Halibut Cove. (The question mark behind each name indicates the uncertainty of the spelling of the word.)

The Soonroodna collection is singularly significant—no other wooden masks, female figure, baby's cradle or wooden staff have been found in Kachemak Country or even elsewhere in Cook Inlet. Pottery is almost as rare. As such, it is truly a unique collection and deserves to be fully documented and appreciated.

Unraveling just a few secrets of Soonroodna has been engaging and satisfying for the author. To better understand Soonroodna, the collection at the Ethnologisches Museum Berlin should be thoroughly analyzed. Some of the information in Jacobsen's book is accurate; some is not. An analysis of the entire collection, object by object, could help clarify that information. Also, archaeologists might be able to determine the location of the lost village by conducting an excavation at the fox farm—but that's another project for another time.

Placing Names with Families and Faces

With the Alaskan acquisition, Americans trickled northward. Naturalists, scientists, explorers, cartographers and others traveled to the new territory to assess and document the resources, as the Russians had done.

A challenging project facing the federal government was to chart the coast of Alaska. Recording existing place names and assigning new names to geographic features was critical for creating accurate charts and maps. In Kachemak Bay, W. H. Dall bestowed at least 19 place names on prominent features during his shoreline surveys in 1880 and 1895. Names which he and others assigned describe

physical features such as Gray Cliff and Mud Bay; reflect a Native origin such as Chugachik and Kasitsna; denote an event such as Battle Creek; identify a natural resource such as Humpy Creek or acknowledge an individual such as Henry (China) Poot who had a connection with a specific place.

Jim Stonehocker of Seldovia lived in the cabin, above, on a bend alongside a meandering creek. Little is known of this man who probably hunted, trapped and fished in China Poot Bay in the 1930s or earlier. Stonehocker (also Stonehaucker and Stonhaucker) was buried in the Seldovia cemetery on May 11, 1939. By 2005, the cabin had collapsed and the trees near it had died and fallen yet the place name, Stonehocker Creek, remains.

Dall named geographic features for people who had a direct connection with Kachemak Bay such as Maxwell Cohen and for some who did not such as Sarah Eldred. *Courtesy of Smithsonian Institution Archives, SA 1145*

William H. Dall

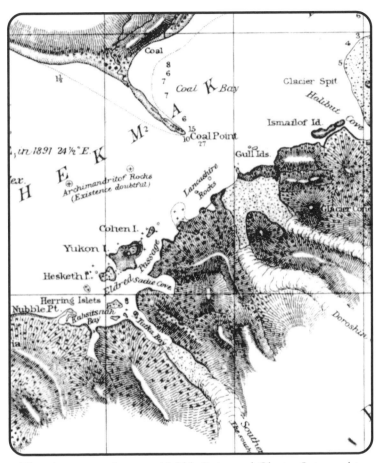

The place names between Nubble Point and Glacier Spit on this section of an 1895 map were bestowed primarily by W. H. Dall. Wosnesenski Glacier is just beyond Doroshin Glacier. Both drain into China Poot Bay, unnamed at that time. *U.S. Geological Survey, 17th Annual Report, Part I, Plate LI*

MAXWELL COHEN
(1844? TO 1894)

National Archives, 22-FA 450, and Nancy Yaw Davis

Taken in 1892, this photograph is labeled, "The agent and his Indian wife, Port Graham, Cook's Inlet." The agent *may be* Maxwell Cohen who managed the Alaska Commercial Company trading post at English Bay from about 1869 until his death.

A newspaper article described him as ". . . sober, industrious and economical, and always had a good salary." His widow and two children returned to Kodiak where Cohen was buried.

As the company agent, Cohen recorded the weather, wind direction, barometric pressure, temperature and usually one or two activities in his daily log book. His main task, however, was to acquire pelts so most entries reflect hunting and trading activities.

June 1883
16th – Party (Native men) returned from Anchor Point. Their catch 14 sea otter.
17th – Bought 7 sea otter skins and 1 brown bear and 2 Caribou(?) skins, Value $223.00.
19th – Bought 1 sea otter and 1 brown bear skin, Value $37.00.
21st – Party out sea otter hunting. Bought 5 sea otter skins and 1 pupp (sic), value $170.

Dall named Cohen Island for this man who had been born in Berlin, Germany, and who was an Alaskan pioneer.

SARAH ELIZABETH ELDRED
(1846 TO 1897)

Sarah (Sadie) Eldred was the wife of Marcus Baker who charted Kachemak Bay in 1880 with Dall. *Drawing by Lee Post from an 1897 photograph*

Born September 2, 1846, at Climax, Michigan, "Sarah Elizabeth Eldred...was totally unlike any other Eldred on record, because of her unusual small size. She was only four-feet one-inch in height when a mature woman, yet she was perfectly proportioned, with bright blue eyes, dark hair, and had a vivacious, dynamic personality. She weighed less than 100 pounds and wore a shoe so small that her shoes had to be made to order." She was affectionately known as "Sadie," "Satie" or "Little Sate."

Sadie attended "Kalamazoo College (Michigan) where her tiny size, striking personality and brilliant mentality made her a center of attention." She may have majored in art for in the college catalog she's listed as a teacher of drawing and painting. She graduated in 1866 near the head of her class.

On December 13, 1874, Sadie married Marcus Baker, a former college classmate, in Climax, Kansas, a community founded by her family after they left Climax, Michigan. The newlyweds moved to Washington, D.C., where he became a lifetime employee of the U.S. Coast and Geodetic Survey.

Sadie died December 29, 1897, in Washington, D.C. Although unable to have children, she was deeply interested in them. Upon her death, "most of her personal estate was bequeathed to a Home for Orphaned Children."

Eldred Passage and Sadie Cove were named in her honor. Today, additional place names include Sadie Peak, Sadie Ridge and the Sadie Knobs. *Quotations courtesy of the Baker family*

SIR THOMAS GEORGE FERMOR-HESKETH
(1849 TO 1924)

Sir Thomas Hesketh, a British yachtsman, posed for this portrait in 1883 three years after he sailed into Kachemak Bay. *Photographic Survey of Private Collections, Courtauld Institute of Art. Image reproduced with permission from Lord Hesketh*

Sir Thomas George Fermor-Hesketh from Lancashire, England, visited Alaska in 1880 specifically to hunt brown bears. On a voyage around the world, the adventurer and big-game hunter sailed into Cook Inlet in May, probably dropped anchor in English Bay to visit the ACC trading post where he would have met Maxwell Cohen, then sailed into Kachemak Bay to take on coal to refuel his yacht, the *Lancashire Witch.*

Two place names acknowledge his brief time in Kachemak Bay: Hesketh Island which commemorates the intrepid traveler himself and Lancashire Rocks, near Neptune Bay, which refer to the *Lancashire Witch.* The yacht ". . . was probably named after the famous but unlucky witches of his native Lancashire," according to Morgan Sherwood.

On another leg of his circumnavigation, the 31-year-old Hesketh sailed to San Francisco where he met and married American heiress Florence Emily, daughter of William Sharon, U. S. senator from Nevada. They moved to England and lived at Rufford Old Hall, seat of the Hesketh family since it was constructed about 1530. Sir Thomas Hesketh was head of the family for 48 years. Two years after his death, his son transferred the Old Hall to The National Trust which manages it today.

W. H. Dall arrived in Kachemak Bay a month after Hesketh's visit. He probably heard about the Englishman from Maxwell Cohen and, subsequently, bestowed those place names on the island and the rocks.

WILLIAM J. MCKEON
(1865 TO EARLY 1920S)

(Place names acknowledging W. J. McKeon were not assigned by Dall.)

Little was known of William J. McKeon until his family contacted the Homer Public Library and, subsequently, the author in 2004.

As best as the family can piece together, McKeon moved to Alaska in 1898, lived in Tyonek then moved to Kachemak Bay. On January 22, 1903, he mailed his family a letter postmarked at Homer. McKeon wrote that he was working as a watchman at the Homer Coal Camp. Possibly, he was the caretaker of the deserted camp near the mines west of present-day Homer. Although the town on the Spit had been abandoned the previous year, the Homer post office remained open in 1903. Stephen Penberthy served as postmaster, as caretaker of the abandoned town and as its sole resident which also suggests that McKeon was not in Homer per se but at the mine camp.

McKeon married Anna Papachka, a Native woman, in 1908. Data in the 1910 U.S. Census indicates that they were living in or near Seldovia. In 1912 he was registered as (hunting) guide #3 by the territorial government. Within the next decade, they had two daughters and two sons. In 1920 they operated a fox farm on Hesketh Island. In the early 1920s William McKeon died and a few years later so did his wife, possibly of tuberculosis. The children were placed in an orphanage until William's brother traveled to Alaska to take them Outside (an Alaskan term indicating the Lower 48 states).

The place names McKeon Flats and McKeon Rock near Neptune Bay were recorded by the U.S. Coast and Geodetic Survey/ U.S. Geological Survey in the 1940s. Later, the name McKeon Spit came into popular use. (Note: in the 1930s when Frederica de Laguna surveyed the coast of Kachemak Bay, she did not mention Neptune Bay. In 1994 when the author asked her about Neptune, the archaeologist said that she was unfamiliar with the name and place.) Maps from the 1930s show that Neptune Bay, as an embayment, did not exist. Most of the area was a grassy flat. On a map from the early 1950s, however, the bay exists and McKeon Spit is identified as a long spit emerging from the eastern shore. (The once-lengthy McKeon Spit had been reduced by water erosion to a mere remnant in 2007.)

Today some residents call the spit which creates China Poot Bay, McKeon Spit.

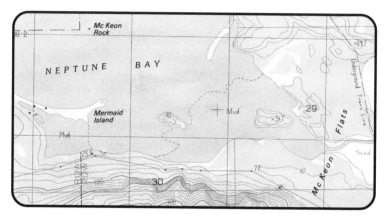

This map of Neptune Bay in 1987 shows McKeon Rock, McKeon Flats and, in the upper middle of the map, a remnant of McKeon Spit. *U.S. Geological Survey, Seldovia quadrangle*

HOMER SPIT STORIES

The Homer Spit is a physically striking natural feature extending outward from the north shore. Stretching northwest to southeast for over four and one-half miles, the tenuous thread of land was relatively unimportant until the late 1880s when coal mining companies used it as a staging area. The deep-water natural harbor on the inside (east side) of the Spit provided, and still provides, safe anchorage for large vessels.

The following represent an eclectic mix of stories about the Spit from one of the earliest descriptions of it to a new chapter in the story of Homer Pennock for whom it was named.

On clear, calm and cold winter days, ice occasionally accumulates on the tide flats along the east shore of the Homer Spit.

THE HISTORY MAKERS

Army Captain John McGilvray was one of the first Americans to explore the Homer Spit. Just one year after the United States purchased Alaska, an aging bark sailed into Kachemak Bay. Aboard the *Torrent* was Captain McGilvray and members of the Second Artillery, Battery F from Fort Vancouver, Washington. (Full story in the chapter "Changing Times, Changing Cultures.") The regiment had been assigned to Alaska to establish a fort in Kenai Harbor, Cook Inlet. Under McGilvray's direction, the *Torrent* sailed into the Gulf of Chugachnik (Kachemak Bay).

Captain McGilvray and several Natives explored the north shore. While seeking a site for the future fort he noted that, ". . . the spit seems to be subject to almost entire overflow, and, perhaps, at extreme high-water, it is entirely inundated. All the main land lying on this harbor and extending several miles into the interior is covered with a species of soft and very wet peat from 3 to 6 feet deep."

Given such conditions, McGilvray decided not to build in the soggy, uninviting land. (How different the history of Homer would have been if a military fort had been the cornerstone of the community.)

It is interesting that the Homer bench was covered with peat.

In 1868, the Little Ice Age was ending which might explain why peat predominated. Few trees grew on the north shore. Fred Anderson, who was a child when his parents and siblings moved to Homer in 1924, told the author decades later that the land was mostly meadow, muskeg and shrubs at that time.

E. De Meulin, First Lieutenant Second Artillery, described exploration of the north shore in these terse journal entries:

July 9. 8 ½ A.M.–Entered Chugachik Bay (Kachemak Bay) and cast anchor in Coal Harbor (Mud Bay). Officers go ashore to select a position. Could not land.

July 10 and 11.–These two days passed in exploring the land to locate the fort. Everywhere rank vegetation. Birch, alder, spruce, cotton trees (cottonwood), currant bushes, fern, etc. No solid ground for foundation–about four feet of peat all over it. Immense quantities of musquitoes (sic). No dry ground. Some ice was found at four feet deep.

July 12, 7 A.M.–We leave Chugachick (sic) for Opasnoy. Thermometer, 59 deg.; barometer, 29.30. Very rough weather. Main sail lost. Return to Chugachick (sic) at 8 ½ P. M.

July 13–Leave Chugachick (sic) at 9 A.M. Strong wind ahead. Tacking across Cook's Inlet.

July 14–Tacking the whole day, with strong wind ahead.

July 15, 6 ¾ A.M.–The boat struck upon the rocks at the entrance of English Harbor (Port Graham harbor), or Opasnoy, and is rapidly filling with water. All the men were saved. We sent an Indian to Kodiak for help.

Tarleton Bean, a fisheries biologist who visited the Spit with Dall, noted enormous quantities of fish, probably herring, stranded by the high tides, great windrows of driftwood, wild wheat, abundant flowers, nesting birds and a little grove of Sitka spruce. Neither Bean nor Dall mentioned people living on the Spit in the summer of 1880.

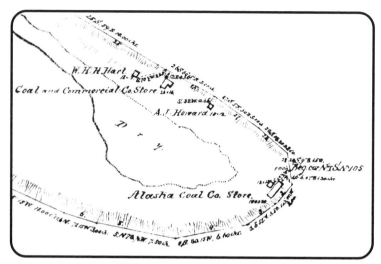

Tip of the Spit in 1892. *Plat of U.S. Survey No. 105*

The 1892 surveys of the unnamed Spit were conducted by Albert Lascy who mapped the entire perimeter in August and September. Near the tip, he drew cabins, stores and several coal storage bunkers. The companies, which were mining near McNeil and Eastland Creeks in the late 1880s and early 1890s, probably utilized the Spit as headquarters.

Lascy illustrated two patches of live spruce and many tree trunks on his lengthy map. The copse of living trees, later known as Green Timbers, slowly died from repeated flooding of their roots after the 1964 earthquake. The last spruce indicated on the 1892 map fell in May 1992, 100 years later.

HOMER PENNOCK
HIS EARLIER LIFE, HIS FIRST WIFE

Homer Pennock was a confidence man, a con man, who acquired money from others through nefarious schemes such as the sale of worthless stocks. Like an unsolved puzzle, tantalizing pieces about this intriguing entrepreneur fall into place occasionally.

Many stories are told about Pennock; some are true, some are not.

Homer Pennock. *Courtesy of Joan Pennock Craig*

He was secretive about himself and his activities, whether past, present or future. Also, it appears that he chose not to correct erroneous information. For example, it was long believed that he was a "Michigan man." Although he conducted business in that state, he was born in New York in 1840 and died there in 1912. Supposedly, Pennock was schooled as a mining geologist and built his career upon the discoveries of mineral ores, the development of legitimate and illegitimate mining companies and the subsequent selling of stock. It appears that fortune slipped into and out of his hands like quicksilver.

An intriguing mystery—What did Homer Pennock look like?—is now solved. As seen here, he looks like a man who exuded a powerful and commanding presence, one who could easily manage a crew of gold miners in the field or a boardroom full of investors. Who wouldn't trust this intelligent-looking, capable mining engineer to safeguard his investments?

Fifty-six-year-old Homer Pennock arrived in Kachemak Country in 1896 as the manager of a crew with the Alaska Gold Mining Company. He established base camp on the sandspit which was soon named for him. Much of what historians know about him comes from several magazine articles written by Della Murray Banks who,

Della Murray Banks, 1898. *Courtesy of Roger Banks*

69

with her husband Austin, accompanied Pennock to Alaska. Pennock promoted the development of a placer gold mine at Anchor Point and although he sought gold throughout Cook Inlet, he failed to find it. When he learned of the gold rush in the Klondike, he departed Alaska, trekked up the Dalton Trail, found no gold yet left his name on Pennock's Post. He retired to New York City with his wife Lilian. When he died, headlines in the Denver Post declared, "Homer Pennock, Once Millionaire, Dies in Poverty."

Erroneous, often conflicting information about Homer Pennock has made research difficult. His New York death certificate, dated July 1912, states that he and Lilian had no children. An obituary note in the *New York Times*, however, states that, "A widow and two sons survive him." The truth was revealed in 1999 when the author talked to Joan Pennock Craig.

Late in life Joan Craig began researching the history of her grandfather, Homer. She contacted the Homer Public Library staff who, in turn, contacted the author. Over several years, Craig and the author shared and compared information and found enough commonalities to verify that Craig's grandfather was, indeed, the very man for whom the town and Spit were named. Joan Craig revealed that her grandfather had been married previously to Annie Hardcastle of Philadelphia and that they had had four children. Two died early in life, yet two sons grew to adulthood and Jerome Humphrey Pennock was Joan's father.

Joan Craig had long sensed that her grandfather was the black sheep of the family for neither her parents nor her beloved grandmother Annie mentioned him often. Also, his career took him away from home for lengthy periods of time. Craig knew nothing about him before his marriage to Annie in 1866. When the author hesitantly mentioned that research indicated that Pennock was a con man, she was not surprised nor dismayed, just eager to learn more. After exchanging information, Joan Craig sent the author the formal portrait of Homer along with photographs of his tombstone in New York City.

In June 2003 Joan Craig visited Alaska and met with the author in Anchorage. Her pursuit of her family history and her willingness to share that information have given Homerites glimpses into other aspects of Pennock's life. And, finally, residents know the looks of the man for whom a town, a Spit and a street were named.

This photograph shows how the coal town of Homer, built in 1899 by the Cook Inlet Coal Fields Company of West Virginia, must have appeared to passengers on ships. The boardwalk, rails, human activity, and sacks probably full of coal, suggest a permanent community. (Although the date in the lower corner appears to be 1907, the author believes that it is actually 1901. The light atop the post causes the one to look like a seven. Homer was abandoned in 1902 and only a caretaker lived there in 1907.) *Collection of the author*

STEPHEN PENBERTHY
HOMER CARETAKER

"Across Kachemak Bay from Seldovia is Homer—another town of the inlet blessed with a poetic name. When I landed at its wharf, in 1905, it was the saddest, sweetest place in Alaska.

We reached it at sunset of a June day.

A low, green, narrow spit runs for several miles out into the waters of the inlet, bordered by a gravelly beach. Here is a railroad…, a telephone line, roundhouses, machine-shops, engines and cars, a good wharf, some of

71

the best store buildings and residences in Alaska, all painted white with soft red roofs, and all deserted!

On this low and lovely spit, fronting the divinely blue sea and the full glory of the sunset, there was only one human being, the postmaster. When the little *Dora* swung lightly into the wharf, this poor lonely soul showed a pitiable and pathetic joy at this fleeting touch of companionship. We all went ashore and shook hands with him and talked to him. Then we returned to our cabins and carried him a share of all our daintiest luxuries.

When, after fifteen or twenty minutes, the *Dora* withdrew slowly into the great Safrano rose of the sunset, leaving him, a lonely, gray figure, on the wharf, the look on his face made us turn away, so that we could not see one another's eyes. It was like the look of a dog who stands helpless, lonely, and cannot follow.

I have never been able to forget that man. He was so gentle, so simple, so genuinely pleased and grateful—and so lonely! . . . one of my most vivid and tormenting memories of Alaska is of a gray figure, with a little pathetic stoop, going up the path from the wharf, in the splendor of that June sunset, with his dog at his side." *Ella Higginson*

Stephen Penberthy. *R. W. Stone Collection, 1904, U.S. Geological Survey*

Stephen Penberthy, the postmaster, caretaker and sole resident of Homer in 1905, must have been the lone and lonely man who Ella Higginson, a writer of Alaskana, described so poignantly. He came to Kachemak Country with Homer Pennock in 1896. When a post office was established on the Spit, Penberthy served as the first postmaster. He probably served until 1907 when mail delivery was discontinued in Homer and routed through Seldovia. Penberthy was also caretaker of the town following its abandonment by the Cook Inlet Coal Fields Company in 1902. He may have left Homer prior to 1910 as his name does not appear on that census.

Pioneer residents of Homer recalled that Henry Ohlson was postmaster in 1913 and Captain Norton from 1922 to 1924. Both men were also caretakers of the deserted town.

A rare photograph taken between 1913 and 1915 shows rails curving around Munson Point and over a bridge crossing Beluga Slough. *Arlan Colton Historic Photograph Collection, PM-2003-5-8, Pratt Museum*

The McAlpin Coal Mining Company owned the town of Homer from about 1904 to 1913. It was, however, unable to obtain patents to the coal claims because President Theodore Roosevelt closed all coal lands in Alaska to entry from 1906 to 1914. McAlpin sold the rolling stock, rails and other equipment to the Miller Machinery Company of Seattle. To obtain lumber to reinforce the railroad bed enough to move the 600 tons of equipment, the company opened a sawmill in Anchorage in 1915, cut and milled trees there, barged them to Homer, and then reinforced the bed.

The railroad equipment was removed from the Homer Spit and shipped Outside between 1913 and 1915.

An engine similar to this may have operated on the Spit from 1899 to 1901. *Drawing by Kay VanDervoort*

What happened to the many buildings in Homer? In 1931 Frederica de Laguna, the archaeologist, photographed them as she

The first wharf and town of Homer on the tip of the Spit, as seen by Frederica de Laguna in 1931, twenty-nine years after they were abandoned. *Collection of the author*

boated passed. Most structures remained intact well into the 1930s. Eventually, some were dismantled and the lumber was reused elsewhere, some deteriorated naturally, a few smaller structures were removed to be reerected elsewhere and some burned in a fire. Supposedly, a small log cabin survived and became part of the Salty Dawg Saloon complex on the Spit.

ON THE LAND—Commercial coaling occurred along the bluffs west of Homer between 1899 and 1950. Because the bluffs are geologically unstable, landslides occur occasionally and can reveal or conceal mining paraphernalia. Occasionally visible are the metal cable used during the 1940s, pieces of cut wood, a few rails and a cluster of stubby pilings in the intertidal area near Bidarka Creek. A coal bunker, represented by the remnant pilings, was in use in 1919. Just when it was constructed, however, remains unknown.

BOGUS BUSINESSES

Near the turn of the twentieth century, two investment schemes were developed locally: one promoted coal and gold mining near Homer and Anchor Point; the other marketed the gold mining camp at Aurora. A third undertaking, the planning of a Finnish colony near Bear Cove, may have been legitimate but that remains to be determined. How did such enterprises function and what characterized them? Historian Ted C. Hinckley wrote that at the outset, investors required "showy, short-range achievements." Quickly, a town, a wharf, a railroad or a post office was constructed—it did not matter what as long as it demonstrated that human activity confirmed "superb investment possibilities."

HOMER-ON-THE-SPIT

Enormous deposits of coal underlie the Kenai Lowland and are visible in the soaring sandstone sea bluffs defining the north shore of Kachemak Bay. Although not the best quality for large scale commercial enterprises, the coal fueled small steamships, heated homes, schools and businesses, stoked cannery machines and provided income for enterprising people who collected and sold it.

Taken from atop a pile driver in 1904, this photograph shows the first town of Homer, a coal company town on the tip of the Spit, two years after it was abandoned. *R.W. Stone Collection, SRW00049, U.S. Geological Survey*

The first town of Homer was built in 1899 by CICF Company which had incorporated in West Virginia. Milled lumber was shipped from the West Coast to construct the 25 to 30 buildings which included a multi-story general mercantile store, a huge wharf, a post office and the accouterments needed to sustain a fully

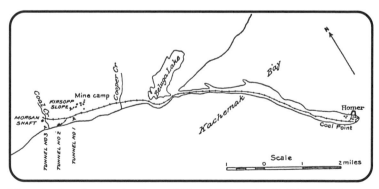

Map of railroad operating from 1899 to 1902. *HM-1979-13-7, Pratt Museum*

76

functioning railroad. Rails stretched for over seven miles along the Spit to the mines near Bidarka Creek (Coal Creek). The town functioned from the autumn of 1899 to March of 1902 and exemplified the intense activity and criteria which, as Hinckley stated, demonstrated "superb investment possibilities."

Fancy stock certificates suggested legitimacy and permanence to the company. *Courtesy of Alaska Rare Coins*

Cook Inlet Coal Fields Company brought men from Outside to manage the town, operate the railroad and mine coal; however, Kenai Peninsula men were also hired. The agricultural experiment station in Kenai needed laborers during the planting and growing season of 1900. When Mr. Nielsen, the agent, tried to hire field hands, he found none available. "The man I thought of hiring left here about three weeks ago. He and all the other white men, about 30 in number, went down to Homer to work for the Cook Inlet Coal [Fields] Company, where they are paying $2.50 per day and board. Under the circumstances I shall have difficulty in hiring men . . . "

Although CICF Company abandoned Homer in 1902, it retained ownership of the town for many years. A caretaker watched over the structures and equipment. Eventually the village was sold but the economic and political climates were not favorable to mining coal until about 1916.

Was Homer a legitimate mining operation or a get-rich-quick scheme? Local lore, passed down for over a century, has maintained that the Spit town and mining operations were fraudulent. People visiting the town also heard similar information. John Kilbuck, a missionary in western Alaska, was aboard a ship heading to the West Coast in 1900 when it stopped at Homer. "Here I saw a railroad, engine and flat cars. I was not impressed particularly, with the coal, for I have mined better looking coal myself. I understand this coal mine, is a grafling (sic) proposition." ('Grafling,' actually 'graftling,' means to acquire money through dishonest or illegitimate means.)

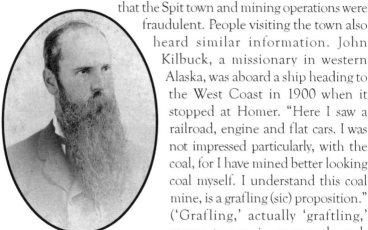

Homer Pennock. *Courtesy of Joan Pennock Craig*

Bogus businesses are usually conceived of and carried out by con men or by organizations fronting for them. Con men are usually intelligent, charismatic and persuasive. Two such men operated in Kachemak Country, H.D. Reynolds and Homer Pennock.

Pennock never actually saw the town which was named for him. It was built two years *after* he left Kachemak Country; however, he and several partners owned stock in CICF and the company was headquartered in Philadelphia where Pennock's first wife lived and where he attended stockholder meetings.

Pennock had a nationwide reputation as the consummate con man. Bruce Cotten, who naively invested in a scam perpetrated by Pennock, spent a miserable winter near Yakutat, Alaska, searching for alleged gold claims. In his book, *An Adventure in Alaska*, Cotten described the genius of Homer Pennock.

". . . Mr. Pennick (sic) is remembered by a large number of other prominent men in this country, who pronounced him the most talented confidence man that ever operated on this continent. His genius in crookedness amounted to greatness, it is said, and even after you know this, it is difficult to withhold your confidence and respect.

"He is described as a faultlessly groomed man with irresistible manners, whose occupation has always been separating American millionaires from some of their hard-earned cash... The man with a few thousand was always safe in his hands, and he is ever ready to help a fellow who is down on his luck.

"Pennick's (sic) genius was for working big game and his power lay in his ability to meet and interest big financiers in his enterprises."

The following article published in a Seattle paper in 1899, described Pennock's methodology. It was published after he left Kachemak Country and before the Cook Inlet Coal Fields Company was incorporated.

WANTS FIFTY THOUSAND
Homer Pennock Sues the Morning Organ.
The Basis for the Suit a Sensational Story Published Last June.

Homer Pennock, a New York promoter and mining man, brought suit today by service against *The* [Seattle] *Post-Intelligencer* for $50,000 damages, which plaintiff alleges he suffered through an alleged false and defamatory article published last June.

The article in question was a description of a fight that was said to have occurred between Senator Green of Mandan, N.D., and one Geo. J. Rennicks, in a room in the Hotel Seattle. Rennicks, it was claimed, got a bad "basting," and following the account of the fight was a good deal of alleged personal history of Rennicks and Homer Pennock. There were such utterances as: "Geo. J. Rennicks, who is said to be a pupil of Homer Pennock, the notorious New York swindler."

"Rennicks' training through his life has been the role of a villain. He has been in the school of Homer Pennock, the notorious New York swindler, who is now said to be in Vienna enjoying the neat sum of $5,000,000 reaped from his Cook Inlet swindles. (The "swindles" may refer to the Anchor Point gold mining camp and/or the selling of coal claims along the north shore of Kachemak Bay.) Pennock, through his man Rennicks, represents that he has the Standard Oil Company back of him and has sold hundreds of claims on Cook Inlet for good round prices which are not worth a dollar.

"He has induced a great many people to go into that country and many of them will be sorely disappointed. Pennock is the man who brought a lot of tin from England about twenty-six years ago and salted a mine on the north shore of Lake Superior. He sold the mine to New York parties for $250,000. They discovered the swindle and Pennock served time in the Toombs prison."

Pennock alleges in his complaint that he was at the time in New York and was on the eve of closing some large deals, but which, through the publication of the story, all failed. His attorney is P.C. Ellsworth of this city.

The author was unable to verify whether Pennock won or lost the lawsuit or if he had reaped $5,000,000 from his swindles in Cook Inlet.

ON THE LAND—Essentially nothing remains of the original town of Homer. A stone monument, identifying the former town site, was erected by citizens in 1967 and is located near the Homer Small Boat Harbor. Local lore claims that a small log building in the Salty Dawg Saloon complex survived from the coal town but that has yet to be verified.

Four buildings comprise the Salty Dawg complex in 2008.
Drawing by Chris Kent, Courtesy Homer Chamber of Commerce

AURORA

Named after the Roman goddess of dawn to symbolize a new beginning in the land of aurora borealis, Aurora was to be the hub of Alaska and Alaska itself the keystone of the Pacific. *Morgan Sherwood*

Aurora Lagoon, located about 12½ miles north and east of Homer, was the site of a bogus gold mining venture in the early 1900s. Conceived by Thomas C. Dunn, the 'false front' of the Aurora Gold Mining Company was cleverly constructed on Aurora Spit. Passengers aboard steamships delivering supplies could visit the warehouse, see the wagon road and telephone poles stretching toward the distant village and leave their mail to be cancelled at the Aurora post office which operated from 1902 to 1904. To the naïve, the facilities and bustling activities on the dock probably suggested similar activity at the camp and mines miles away. The actual town, or the "non-town" as Sherwood called it, was conveniently located out-of-sight, about a mile south and east of the dock and warehouse which were on Aurora Spit.

When the gold did not pan out, Dunn tried to sell Aurora as the southern terminus for a railroad into the interior of Alaska. But, by 1902, Dunn was done with

U.S. Geological Survey, Seldovia quadrangle map

Aurora. His successor, H. D. Reynolds, was a shareholder in Dunn's enterprise. (Sherwood reported his name as Henry Derr Reynolds; Hinckley reported it as Harry D. Reynolds. Such discrepancies in the names of people and companies were not uncommon.) Reynolds arrived at Aurora in 1902 to investigate the business for some investors. Displeased with what he learned, he acquired and tried to resuscitate the ailing company which he renamed the Reynolds-Alaska Development Corporation.

The promotional literature captioned these photographs: "Bunk house, store and boarding houses at the Aurora Mines." Are there four buildings as implied or two photographed from different angles in different seasons and where are the chimneys? *Courtesy of Morgan Sherwood*

Claude Cane, a British big-game hunter, was aboard the *Bertha* when it tied up at the dock on the Aurora Spit in 1902. He watched as heavy machinery was offloaded for gold mining. Remnants of that machinery, delivered over a century ago, remain fairly intact on private property on Aurora Spit.

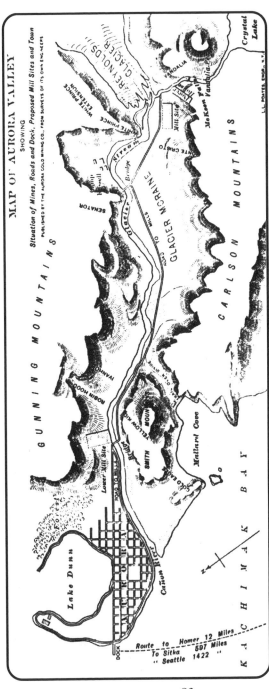

The second promoter of Aurora, H. D. Reynolds, used his skills as a former advertising manager to create a prospectus to sell Aurora. On his map, Lake Dunn is actually Aurora Lagoon, Canon River is Portlock Creek and Reynolds Glacier is Portlock Glacier. Some place names are perplexing. Why would Reynolds, promoting a nefarious activity, name a gold mine after Robin Hood, the legendary outlaw of Sherwood Forest who stole from the rich and gave to the poor? More appropriate perhaps was the moniker of another mine, Monte Cristo, probably named after the barren island in the Mediterranean Sea where a fictional Count discovered treasure. Surely the promoter of Aurora identified with the 'Count' for he was hoping to discover his treasure in Alaska. *Courtesy of Morgan Sherwood*

Reynolds was another candidate for the title of "the most talented confidence man in North America." Sherwood described him as Alaska's "most colorful and charismatic stock hustler." Like Homer Pennock, Reynolds was East Coast born and educated, self-confident and highly skilled at convincing others to part with their money. At different times in their lives, both men were wealthy and penniless. They operated in Kachemak Bay five years apart.

H. D. Reynolds was the ultimate hustler, so smooth and convincing that he totally deceived John G. Brady, Alaska's Governor from 1897 to 1906. "I believe that Reynolds is honest. . . ," the Governor avowed. In his annual gubernatorial report, Brady included a description of Aurora written by Reynolds. By allowing Reynolds to publish in the report, Brady tacitly endorsed him and his company. As Homer Pennock had invoked the name of Standard Oil Company in his promotions, so Reynolds invoked the name of Alaska's Governor.

Courtesy of Alaska Rare Coins

Governor Brady's signature on stock certificates and his title as Resident Alaskan Director of the Reynolds-Alaska Development Company lent invaluable credibility and respectability to the

84

shenanigans at Aurora.

Ralph W. Stone, U.S. Geological Survey geologist, visited Aurora Spit on June 20, 1904. He saw exactly what others wanted him to see. His field notes mentioned ". . . a house and wharf with warehouse on it where steamers land goods for a proposed mining camp. A telephone line and road run inland to [a] village about a mile back at [the] mouth of a canyon. On [the] wharf were parts of a stamp mill, dynamo, and other machinery, wire, cables, coal, bidarka, etc. Three dories in lagoon back of house." The geologist also referred to a "Dozen or 15 houses, some 2-storied. Watchman lives there. But large amount of material was brought in before mining expert was consulted. Rumor says he told them to 'find your mine first.'"

H.D. Reynolds. *Courtesy of Morgan Sherwood*

Did Stone actually visit the village site or did he assume that it existed because the dock, warehouse and post office existed? It is difficult to tell from his field notes. He failed to comment on whether or not gold was present in the mines, which suggests that he did not visit them.

Interestingly, Stone noted that the mining camp was "proposed." Proposed in 1904? Supposedly it had been operating during the previous two to three years.

Even with the Governor's strong endorsement, Reynolds was unable to sustain his golden dreams. Investments soured and dwindled and Reynolds shifted his entrepreneurial expertise to Prince William Sound. There he promoted the development of several copper mines and, in 1907, purchased a large part of the town of Valdez; however, his health and wealth diminished rapidly. The following year he was committed to a mental hospital. Eight years later the indefatigable investor was back in Alaska, promoting the construction of a copper smelter in Seward. Financial support was scarce and the smelter never was built.

Was there gold at Aurora? G. C. Martin, U.S. Geological Survey geologist, surveyed much of Kachemak Bay in 1911. His notes state that three mines were driven into a fractured zone in graywacke near the contact with a 20-foot dike of porphyry. Small amounts of pyrite, often called fool's gold, were reported in the rocks lying in dump heaps near the mines. Apparently, no gold was observed; however, it's unknown whether or not Martin actually visited the mines.

Despite all the hype and hyperbole, Aurora probably never functioned as a village. Tom Shelford, who moved to Seldovia in 1926 and later to Homer, remembered hearing that Aurora was a stock promotion deal; that the promoters bought mining equipment, dumped it on the beach, then went south with all the money. Frank C. Churchill, a Land Office employee in Alaska and occasional visitor to Kachemak Bay, reported, "There is no town of Aurora and the only thing I know of [that] it has to sell there is water power, unless it be hot air."

The similarities between Homer and Aurora are intriguing. Both beautifully exemplified Hinckley's axiom. The publicly visible and accessible areas of each town were located on spits, at water's edge where steamships could dock; and, at both sites, wires strung on poles suggested the presence of a telephone or telegraph system. Whether or not they were functional remains unknown. Also, Homer and Aurora had a post office which functioned for years after the communities were abandoned. Equally important, the actual mines were remote from the scrutinizing eye of the public. In Homer, cars filled with coal were parked near the roundhouse and dock, in part because small quantities were actually sold, but possibly also for show. The author wonders if samples of gold were displayed in the warehouse at Aurora.

ON THE LAND—What evidence of Aurora exists on the land? In 1991 Peter Zollars and the author explored the remnant dock and the rusting stamp mill and dynamo then followed the line of deteriorating telephone poles to the alleged village site. There, they found rusted nails, shards of windowpane and bottle glass, gun and rifle cartridges (some contemporary), pieces of porcelain, bricks and little else. There were no building foundations, nothing to suggest a viable functioning town with 12 to 15 houses and offices. They also spent many tedious hours forcing their way through the dead and downed spruce which obliterated the wagon road leading to Portlock Creek. (The late Sewell "Stumpy" Faulkner, of Aurora and Anchorage, told the author that one could walk the wagon road to the creek until a heavy blow-down obliterated it in 1981.) When Zollars and the author arrived on the bank of the creek they saw the mine opening across the roaring waters but found no evidence of the bridge or any other man-made features.

In 1989, the *tip* of Aurora Spit and land abutting the southern end of Aurora Lagoon, including the former town site, were designated part of Kachemak Bay State Park.

PORT AXEL

Bear Cove, north of Aurora, was the site of a proposed agricultural community. The future colony was named Port Axel for its promoter, Axel Hornberg, a Finnish-American shipping company executive headquartered in New York. The residents, to be immigrants from Finland, would develop the fisheries and the agricultural and mineral resources near the head of Kachemak Bay.

To learn more about the resources and development potential, Hornberg sent Adam Widenius, J. W. Friedman and Oscar Ullman to explore Kachemak Bay in 1905-1906. In Bear Cove, the newcomers built at least one cabin, hewed a right of way through the forest and supposedly made other improvements.

Widenius carefully noted the presence of coal in the north shore bluffs, gold placer mining near Anchor Point, fish and wildlife and good grazing land for cattle. He also photographed the resources. Widenius sent his report and pictures to Lars and Axel Krogius in Finland, business associates who took over after Axel Hornberg died in December 1905. Although the reports should have stimulated an influx of immigrants, no Finns ever came. The Finnish colony was finished before it really began.

Was Port Axel another bogus business? Elsa Pedersen and Richard Pierce wrote that, ". . . Widenius did not try to picture the

Port Axel enterprise as a get-rich-quick scheme." On the other hand, W. A. Langille, who visited Kachemak Country in 1904, strongly suggested that it was another spurious enterprise whose ". . . evident purpose is stock jobbing and would bear investigation."

Port Axel faded into a historic footnote yet the twenty-two photographs at the Pratt Museum provide a glimpse of Kachemak Country over a century ago.

A successful moose hunter in 1905 or 1906. *Adam Widenius Historic Photograph Collection, PM-1994-68-19, Pratt Museum*

FARMING FOXES

Fox fever flew through Kachemak Country in the first three decades of the twentieth century. When residents discovered that fox fur was fashionable throughout Europe and America and that foxes with high quality fur could be raised in Kachemak Country, a new economy developed.

"Alaska, and especially Cook Inlet, is particularly adapted to the raising of silver fox," wrote F. W. Williamson, a fox farmer from Kasilof, in "The Pathfinder of Alaska" in 1925. "The climate conditions are ideal and feed is easily obtained. The Inlet and lakes are full of scrap fish which is excellent for fox feed if fed with judgment

and the weather is generally good at the time of year that the pups are born. The winters are long and even and produce a coat of fur excelled no place in the world. Above all else the Alaska fox has not been inoculated with the numerous diseases that cause so much grief and loss among breeders in the states."

People settling along the coast of Kachemak Bay quickly immersed themselves in the new economy. Territorial records show

that Arctic foxes were farmed on Hesketh and Yukon Islands as early as 1900, marking the formal beginning of the industry in Cook Inlet. Fox farming caught on like wildfire racing through dry timber, particularly after World War I.

Courtesy of Ed Bailey

Two species of foxes inhabit Alaska: red, above, and Arctic fox. Red foxes occupy most of the state and were bred to obtain silver, cross and black color phases. Regardless of their color phase, reds usually have a white-tipped tail. Arctic foxes inhabit coastal Alaska from Bristol Bay north and eastward into Canada. A white and a blue color phase occur. The blue phase was preferred in Kachemak Country.

Several people are credited with starting fox farming locally. Joe Filardo (also Filardeau) and John Herbert, who lived at the head of Kachemak Bay about 1909, live-trapped wild reds for their breeding stock. Newton P. Shular and his wife, Ida Hosea, moved to Anchor Point in 1912 to start fox ranching. They live-trapped animals in the Caribou

Newton P. Shular. *Courtesy of Newton P. Shular Family*

and Sheep Hills. Their Anchor Point Silver Fox Farm was managed by J. L. Waller of Anchorage and "...produced for its owner a profit of over $50,000," according to an article in the *Anchorage Daily Times* in 1922. Shular bred silver grey foxes and pure black foxes, producing most unusual and relatively rare pelts which he personally marketed Outside. A prime pair of foxes could bring as much as $2,400. In 1919, Shular sold the highly successful farm to a company headed by J.L. Waller, his former manager, and a David F. Donegan. Although on paper Shular sold the farm for a good price, his daughter wrote to the author that the buyers suffered financial setbacks and never fully paid Shular what they owed.

INTRODUCTION OF FOXES ON SELECT ISLANDS IN KACHEMAK BAY

Island	Species	Year stocked
Aurora	Arctic fox and red fox	1929
Cohen	Arctic fox	1920
Herring	Arctic fox	1921
Hesketh	Arctic fox and red fox	1900 and 1929 respectively
Ismailof	Arctic fox	1929
McKeon	Arctic fox	1929
Passage	Arctic fox	1916
Yukon	Arctic fox	1900

Source: Ed Bailey

Fox farming was labor intensive. Farmers were tied closely to their animals and the land and success depended upon the time, energy, efforts and money they expended. Although many residents owned one or more pairs, those who devoted their entire energies to fur farming made it a local success. Some people raised foxes for their pelts, others as breeding stock to sell.

The Sholin men, who lived near Homer, were also pioneer fox farmers. "When one thinks silver black fox and Cook Inlet, he generally thinks of Andrew and Ed Sholin. In my opinion, to these two are mostly due the phenomenal success of the industry in this district," wrote Williamson. "The Sholin Bros. trapped their foxes in the Sheep and Caribou Hills and installed them on a ranch near Homer. The first year (1915), they didn't have any success . . . However . . . (in 1917) they had a very good increase. They have had success ever since. They sold pups as breeders at a price easily met by all and not only that but were always willing to tell a new beginner. . . all they knew about raising foxes. I am sure that many of my fellow ranchers can always look back to Andrew and Ed Sholin with gratitude."

In the early 1920s, the largest fur market in the world, Funston Bros. & Co., of St. Louis, Missouri, paid $375 to $500 for a prime silver fox pelt and $125 to $160 for a prime blue fox pelt. Even more valuable were pairs of foxes known to be successful breeders. At the peak of the fur industry in Southcentral Alaska, a prime breeding pair might be worth several thousand dollars.

John Herbert holds two foxes on his Passage Island farm near Port Graham in the late 1910s or 1920s. Below: Steve Zawistowski. *Both photographs Steve Zawistowski Collection. Collection of the author*

Good nutrition was essential for raising animals with superior coats. Free or inexpensive meat was relatively easy to obtain in Kachemak Country. Fish offal from herring salteries and salmon canneries along with meat from seals, porpoise and beluga were fed to the omnivores. Surplus meat was canned. Clams, mussels, birds and eggs were utilized as food also. Steve Zawistowski, who farmed at Battle Creek and Martin River between 1930 and 1932, often visited the Fox River Flats. There, he would locate tern or gull nests, remove all but one egg and then prop a small alder branch alongside the nest for future reference. The birds would continue to lay eggs and he would continue to gather them. Zawistowski also remembered a California man who killed large whales and sold the meat to fox farmers.

Did fox farmers kill moose for food? "No old-time fox farmer would ever *admit* to feeding moose meat to the foxes, but many did. A man who had worked for Harry (Leonardt) and Paddy (Patterson) for several years told us they killed at least 40 moose every winter and sometimes nearly twice that many," wrote Elsa Pedersen who, with her husband, Ted, lived near Leonardt and Patterson's Bear Cove fox farm in the late 1940s and 1950s.

Women and children often killed small animals to help feed foxes. Lillian Walli, of Stariski and Homer, remembered the incredible populations of porcupines and rabbits during the 1920s and 1930s and how easy it was for her and her friends to kill them. John Herbert, who raised blues on Passage Island from 1916 into the 1920s, paid Larry and Micky Moonin of Port Graham, 25¢ per rabbit and 50¢ per porcupine. On a good day, the boys would snare 10 rabbits and 20 porcupines.

The fox farm on Passage Island near Port Graham operated between 1916 and 1933 making it one of the longer running operations in Kachemak Country. Large clean pens, sizeable nesting boxes and owners devoted to the welfare of their animals contributed toward the longevity and success of this farm shown here in 1920. *Steve Zawistowski Collection. Collection of the author*

Greens were fed to foxes also. In 1932, Frederica de Laguna excavated a site on Yukon Island. Bill Newman, a student at Haverford College, Haverford, Pennsylvania, was a member of her field crew. As he recalled, "...all the people that were raising foxes. . . raised lettuce. It was proven fact or a tradition, at least, that the fox would mate more effectively in the spring if they were fed lettuce hay. Lettuce was a commodity not for us to eat but [it] turned out

J.L. Swank raised foxes in China Poot Bay into the 1930s. *Historic documents, PM-2005-30-1, Pratt Museum*

[that] since it was so readily available, we had lettuce."

A fox farm could be as elaborate or as simple as money and materials allowed. Some became a conglomerate of pens and specialized buildings. Chicken wire pens, of all sizes, housed breeding pairs, pregnant females, vixens with kits and diseased animals. Structures served as grain storage sheds, smokehouses in which to preserve meat, cookhouses in which to cook daily meals of meat and grains, and pelting sheds in which to kill the foxes and process and store their skins.

The killing and pelting of foxes occurred in winter when their fur was thick and luxurious. Usually all but the breeding pairs were killed and their hides were tanned, stretched and stored. Zawistowski and his partners boated bundles of pelts from their Battle Creek farm to Seldovia. From there furs were shipped to Seattle then London. Payment arrived months later. Zawistowski said a pelt averaged about $100 in 1931. When the industry collapsed, a pelt was valued at only $11.

The rearing of foxes on islands was popular along the south shore. Blues do not swim great distances so they were released on sizeable islands to reproduce. They scavenged for food, devoured carrion, clams and mussels, berries, and eggs, chicks and adult birds. Although sometimes money could be saved by releasing foxes on islands, farmers often needed to haul fresh water, supplement their food and install traps to catch the animals.

Kachemak Country was the center of the fur farming industry in Southcentral Alaska from about 1922 to 1932. Headquartered in Seldovia were the Seldovia Fox Breeders Association and the Cook Inlet Blue and Black Fox Farmers Association. The latter had 52 registered members in 1925, making it the largest membership organization in Cook Inlet.

Tables, below, show the names of fox farmers, approximate dates they operated and the number of pairs they owned during that time. The information appears as published in the territorial records; thus, there are some mistakes. The list is not inclusive; for example, farmers at Anchor Point are not mentioned. Also, when a person such as Steve Zawistowski bought into an existing business, his name might not appear on official documents.

HOMER AREA, MILLERS LANDING AND EAST END ROAD

Alfred Anderson and Jane Flindahl	1924-1928	6 pair silvers
Gustav Anderson	ca.1924-1936	6 pair silvers and blues
C. W. Harrington	ca. 1925-1930	6 pair silvers and blues
Henry and Lee Olsen and Mrs. Woodard	1919-1935	17 pair silvers
J. W. Palmer	ca. 1925-1930	6 pair silvers
Sam Pratt	1931-1936	8 pair silvers
Stanton Shafer	ca. 1923-1931	8 pair silvers
Andrew, Carl, Ed Sholin	1915-1934	30 pair silvers
Frank and John Sodeburg	ca. 1921-1926	8 pair silvers
Charles Miller	ca. 1925-1930	7 pair blues
Jack Dietz	1926-1932	7 pair blues
Karl and Stanley Nielson	1925-1933	12 pair silvers
Henry Wells	1922-1929	4 pair silvers

EASTLAND CREEK TO AURORA

Harry White	ca. 1925-1930	12 pair silvers
Hjlmer Olsen	1922-1932	12 pair silvers
H.T. Jansen	1922-1934	10 pair silvers
Leonhardt and Patterson	ca. 1918-1936	20 pair silvers
Axel Johnson	ca. 1920-1928	12 pair silvers

HALIBUT COVE TO KASITSNA BAY

F. J. Munson	ca. 1929	blue foxes
Dan Peterson	ca. 1923-1928	6 pair silvers
Pete Olsen	ca. 1920-1929	blue foxes
Tollok Ollestad	1922- ca.1930	blue foxes
Burgin & Pollard	ca. 1925-1929	blue foxes
"Snuess" Nelson	1926-1930	6 pair silvers
Louis Huber	1928-1932	blue foxes
Keith McCullough	1921-1926	blue foxes

SELDOVIA TO ENGLISH BAY

T. Lloyd	ca. 1925-1928	5 pair blues
Frank Raby	1923-1926	mink
John Herbert and Tollok Ollestad	1916-1922	blue foxes
John Herbert and Dr. Spalding	1922-1928	blue foxes
Bob Smith	1929-1933	blue foxes

Source: John Robert Huston

The fox farming industry provided several decades of employment for Kachemak residents. From Passage Island to the Fox River Flats to Anchor Point, the coastal wilderness was inhabited. Residents had created a successful economy from a local resource. But fashion is fickle. As fox coats, capes, muffs and hats dropped out of favor in Europe, they were replaced by beaver fur accessories. In America, the Great Depression of the 1930s and drop in demand for luxuries also contributed to the collapse of fur farming. By the close of the 1930s, most Kachemak farmers had pelted off permanently. Those who quit found other careers. Steve Zawistowski ran a trap line at the head of Kachemak Bay for 13 winters and fished for salmon in the summers, among other jobs.

Many fox farmers entered the fisheries. Then as now, residents took jobs not necessarily for the love of the job but simply to remain in Kachemak Country. As those with a passionate love of the land have said, and still say, "I'll do whatever it takes to make a living so long as I can remain here."

SALTING HERRING, TRAPPING SALMON

The marine riches of Kachemak Bay are legendary. This was once a bay of seemingly endless bounty. The carbon-rich, cold waters teemed with commercial quantities of halibut and herring, salmon and shrimp and crab. Not so long ago, unusually large herring wintered in deep embayments, hundreds of harbor seals lazed on sand beaches and belugas splashed and flashed white in emerald waters. The abundant marine life was attracted by lengthy food webs in unsullied waters.

The healthy, hearty populations of fish beckoned residents and non-residents to develop the

fisheries, and they did. Although seemingly remote and isolated, Kachemak fishermen and their livelihoods were strongly connected to events and economies outside of Alaska, as they still are.

When Lance Trasky posited a question in the title of his 1982 article, "Kachemak Bay-the richest bay in the world?," he answered it by listing commercially important species such as crab, shrimp, halibut, herring, salmon, octopus and clams. The Alaska Department of Fish and Game biologist then provided select catch and harvest statistics along with wholesale values for several fisheries to document the "richness" of Kachemak Bay. He suggested that "...on a per acre basis (Kachemak Bay) may be the most productive fishery habitat in the State of Alaska." He closed his article, however, with an ominous warning: "...if development in the Bay *continues* at the current rate without adequate consideration for fish and wildlife resources and habitats, there will *continue to be* a slow, and probably imperceptible decline in the productivity of the Bay, which ultimately will be reflected in smaller catches of fish and shellfish, and fewer numbers of wildlife."

Less than 20 years after Trasky asked if Kachemak Bay were the richest in the world, the commercial fisheries for king, Tanner and Dungeness crab, Pandalid shrimp, the large herring and for some clam species had been closed for years and many salmon runs had been enhanced artificially.

At the beginning of the twentieth century, no one could have imagined the mercurial rise and precipitous decline of the herring fishery and the lengthy tenure and politically driven demise of the salmon trap fishery.

Herring and salmon are very different species requiring different types of fisheries. These dissimilar fish, one species which wintered in Kachemak Bay and the other which summered there, formed the economic backbone for the development of the regional fisheries.

THE HERRING HARVESTERS

Herring are one of the most important food fishes in the world. With over 180 species, they provide tons of food annually for consumption by people, marine mammals, birds, invertebrates and other fish. Not only are the silvery-sided hoards harvested but, in some fisheries, so are their roe or eggs.

When the great schools of herring returned from the open ocean to winter in Kachemak Bay about 1911, close behind came the herring harvesters—West Coast fleets including fishermen, gibbers, packers and company managers. Crowding the waterways were wooden schooners converted to processing plants, small steamers to transport fish, scows to haul away fish waste and wooden dories made locally and used by area fishermen. The companies managed all aspects of the late winter or spring fishery and, when the harvest ended, the catch and crew returned to the West Coast. Over time, however, men and women chose to stay in Kachemak Country and communities like Halibut Cove, Seldovia and Homer grew.

Men haul in a three-inch-mesh gill net in Halibut Cove Lagoon in 1917. After 1923, purse seining was permitted.
Tousley Collection, Anchorage Museum

The herring fishery created a seasonal boom and bust economy, especially in Halibut Cove and Seldovia. According to Jack English, a Seldovian from 1923 until his death in 1989, "Seldovia was first of all a herring town." The Russian place name, *Seldevoy*, which appeared on an 1852 chart, is translated as 'herring bay.' Processing plants and support facilities, stretching along the waterfront, allowed for the full development of the regional fishing fleet which, over the decades, pursued not only herring but also salmon, crab and shrimp.

The community of Halibut Cove and the herring fishery developed simultaneously, according to Clem Tillion, a Cove resident since the late 1940s. Great schools of herring wintered in Halibut Cove Lagoon and nearby embayments along the south shore.

This metal barrelhead stencil was found on a beach in Halibut Cove. *Courtesy of Marti and Rick Anderson*

Herring were processed on ships or in shorefast plants called salteries (also saltries). Large ships such as the *Rosamond* and *San Salvador* were converted into processing plants. The ships functioned like small communities. Stanley Nielsen, a Homer boy during the herring boom, vividly remembered the lights of the floating salteries twinkling golden on the cold, dark winter waters of Kachemak Bay—a shining symbol of the silvery riches being harvested from the bay.

To build the salteries, docks, mess halls, bunk houses and other structures, hills were stripped of spruce. Large salteries were sprinkled on Ismailof Island, in Halibut Cove Lagoon, and in Tutka and Seldovia Bays. They were often perched atop log pilings over the intertidal zone. Offal was shoveled through holes in the floor onto the beaches where the daily tides would flush it away, but only when the water was high enough to reach it. A handful of smaller, locally owned plants also existed, including one on the Homer Spit. Numerous businesses developed to support the fishery.

The San Juan Saltery in Tutka Bay was dismantled by Ted Pedersen in 1946 or 1947. He hauled some of the lumber to his home in Bear Cove then sold the rest to pay for his winter's grubstake. According to local lore, the 70-by-100-foot structure was converted to a salmon cannery after the demise of the herring fishery. *Theodore Pedersen Historic Photograph Collection, PM-1997-60-139, Pratt Museum*

Midwest and West Coast markets preferred salted or pickled fish so the Kachemak catch was usually salted, packed in wooden barrels then shipped to the appropriate markets. In the United States, the Scotch-cure method of salting herring was practiced only in Alaska. This method required strictly fresh, blemish-free, well-drained fish which were processed immediately upon transport to the salteries. The unusually large herring, up to 15 inches, worked well for this type of processing.

ALBIN "ROSIE" ROSENBLAD
HERRING FISHERMAN

Born in 1887 on an island between Sweden and Finland, Albin "Rosie" Rosenblad went to sea as a young man and eventually found himself in Alaska. In 1925 he was working in a herring saltery in Halibut Cove. "And when I came up here I said that's as far as I go."

During the seasonal fishery, Rosenblad worked as a gibber. To gib a fish for Scotch-curing, he would have held

101

it in one hand and with a swift, skillful single stroke of a knife, removed its throat, pectoral fins, gills, guts, heart and liver. The cleaned fish was then placed in a brine of rousing salt. After being soaked for a prescribed time, it was packed in a barrel. Gibbers earned $1.00 per barrel. Although he could pack four to five barrels a day, he fell short of the Scottish women who could pack twice as many.

In Halibut Cove, Rosenblad built a comfortable cabin and occupied it for over four decades. Like other residents, he tended a bountiful garden, hunted moose and waterfowl, dug clams, fished and heated his cabin with coal from the north shore. He also washed everything down with home brew which he made regularly and sometimes aged ". . . as long as overnight!"

Rosenblad was picking salmon from his nets well after his 80 birthday. He died in Sitka in 1972. The place name, "Rosie's Bight," honors his memory and identifies his home cove. *From original by Morgan Sherwood*

Albin Rosenblad, in 1968, holds a painting of himself, center, with Jacob "Rusty" Lien, on his left, and Slim Taeschner, on his right. *Elmer F. Sundsby Collection, Archives and Special Collections Department, Consortium Library, University of Alaska Anchorage*

As the fisheries developed, so did boat building. Builders scoured the forests for the perfect spruce trunk from which to remove a plank or a plank with an attached root. Planks were then cut vertically into identically shaped ribs to frame a dory. Today, very few living trees remain that show the scars where planks were removed.

Jack English vividly recalled the abhorrent waste of herring in Seldovia. Fish were so plentiful and the catches so great that often boats could scarcely stay afloat. Saltery foremen became so selective that they accepted only the very best and dumped the rest. Discarded fish and offal accumulated on beaches, often so thick that the tides were unable to move the stinking, gelatinous mass. Once clogged with hoards of healthy herring, waterways became choked with their rotting remains which smothered the vegetation and robbed oxygen from the water. The befouling of beaches affected everyone; but, as Jack English stated, "When the beach was smelling, the cash register was ringing." In Kachemak Country

Viewed from the bow of a boat, the saltery near the Saddle Trail in Halibut Cove is shown in an undated photograph, top, and in 2002, bottom. *Top: Elmer F. Sundsby Collection, Archives and Special Collections Department, Consortium Library, University of Alaska Anchorage*

the ringing of the cash register was sweet music indeed for almost 20 years.

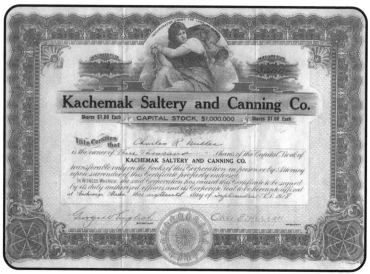

The sale of stock certificates helped support the fishery. *Courtesy of Alaska Rare Coins*

Herring spawned at Port Graham, Seldovia Bay, MacDonald Spit, Tutka Bay, Halibut Cove, Ismailof Island, Mallard Bay, Aurora Lagoon, Bear Cove, Kasitsna Bay and on the Homer Spit.

As the fishery ended each spring, surviving herring moved into shallow waters to spawn. Females deposited their sticky eggs on vegetation and males covered them with milt. George Rounsefell, a fisheries biologist, described the phenomenon in May 1926: "As soon as the tide commenced to fall they approached the shore and rippled the surface as they swam restlessly about. When the tide was about a quarter out they commenced to spawn all around the shores of the lagoon (Kasitsna Bay) in the eel grass which grew abundantly about a foot in length. Many, left stranded by the falling tide, were being devoured by thousands of sea gulls that had gathered as if by magic. At first the herring spawned only around the shores, but when the tide had fallen farther, they spawned over the entire floor of the lagoon which at low tide was covered with about two feet of water and carpeted luxuriously with eel grass."

Unlike salmon, herring do not die after spawning. Those not devoured by flocks of frenzied birds and hoards of hungry seals, sea lions and beluga, returned to the open ocean.

In the early 1930s the great schools of silver herring, which had turned briefly into gold, were gone. The huge herring failed to return. When the fishery collapsed, it did so quickly. Increased competition from foreign fleets, newly developed herring fisheries elsewhere and a lack of conservation measures contributed to the decline. Following the collapse, the huge herring never returned to Kachemak Bay. What happened to them remains a mystery.

The salteries remained silent, the residents resigned yet resilient for dwelling in Kachemak Bay were pods of crab, great schools of shrimp and, in summer, five species of Pacific salmon.

THE SALMON HARVESTERS

Stanley and Karl Nielsen packed silver salmon bellies in salt barrels to sell to Outside markets in the 1920s. *Ken Branch Historic Photograph Collection, PM-2005-19-14, Pratt Museum*

People living along the coast of Alaska have harvested salmon for thousands of years. Many rivers, streams, even creeklets of Cook

Inlet support runs of king (Chinook), silver (coho), red (sockeye), pink (humpback) and chum (dog) salmon. The fish spend their developing years at sea then return to their natal waterways at maturation. Each species returns at a slightly different time although migrations occasionally overlap.

The first salmon fish traps on the West Coast were installed in 1861 in the Sacramento River. Less than two decades later, modified traps were in use in Alaska. (The commercial salmon canning industry in Cook Inlet actually began prior to the herring fishery.) Along the wide and lengthy beaches of the Kenai Peninsula, from Bluff Point near Homer to beyond Kenai, salmon traps achieved their full potential. The configuration of beaches and the daily flooding and ebbing of tides allowed for the extensive development of the Kenai Peninsula fishery. Twice in every 24 hours and 50 minutes, the beaches are flooded; twice in that same length of time, the water ebbs and the beaches are left dry and accessible to fishermen.

As with the herring fishery, West Coast companies promoted and developed the salmon trap fishery. The Alaska Packing Company (later the Alaska Packers Association) of San Francisco pioneered the Cook Inlet salmon canning industry when it opened a plant at the mouth of the Kasilof River in 1882. Less than two decades later, APA operated eight fish traps and the Pacific Steam Whaling Company at Kenai operated five along Kenai Peninsula beaches. (Victor Holm, a resident of Kasilof from 1890 to 1944, managed the Alaska Packers trap near Stariski Creek north of Anchor Point for many years.) Unable to depend upon the few and widely scattered residents of the Peninsula, companies usually brought a full compliment of equipment and employees to the Kenai for the season.

Salmon traps were effective in part because salmon behavior is relatively predictable. As great schools migrated back to their birth streams or lakes, those that swam along the shore of the Peninsula encountered one fish trap after another. Like cattle fences, the wooden and wire (or webbing) structures stopped their forward movement and forced them to turn outward, away from the shore. Directed by the poles and webbing, the salmon swam into a v-shaped opening which led them into the heart of the trap. As the

An aerial photograph shows the configuration of a fish trap near Seldovia in 1956. *Richard W. Tyler Historic Photograph Collection, PM-2001-14-4, Pratt Museum*

tide ebbed, fishermen tossed the fish into their skiffs then delivered them directly to the canneries or to cannery-owned boats waiting nearby. Canneries operated in such places as Kasilof and Kenai, Portlock and Port Graham, Seldovia and on the Homer Spit.

Two types of traps existed: hand-driven traps and pile-driven traps. Hand-driven or hand traps were constructed of small spruce poles pounded manually into the beach sediments then wired together to create the trap fence. These smaller traps were often owned and operated by residents. Ero Walli and Lillian Lingstrang, who married in 1919 and homesteaded near Stariski, operated a trap for several decades. They sold their catches to Whitney-Fidalgo or to Alaska Year 'Round cannery in Seldovia. A 50-pound king salmon often earned them 25¢, for the entire fish.

Residents who owned hand traps usually removed the pilings at the end of summer to save for another season; if not, they risked having the pilings destroyed by ice or weakened by teredo worms.

The huge pile-driven traps, however, were relatively permanent structures constructed of tall, de-limbed spruce logs pounded into the beach by a mechanical pile driver. These traps often extended hundreds of feet outward from shore. Pile traps were usually owned by non-Alaskan companies. Before winter, the fencing material was removed yet the poles were left in place.

Residents found a variety of jobs associated with the fishery such as cutting and preparing spruce logs as pilings and then hauling and installing them at trap sites. Tom Larson, who moved to Halibut Cove in 1957 near the end of the fishery, cut trap poles at his sawmill. Residents also worked at the traps, in the canneries or fished from their boats for the companies.

Salmon traps were highly controversial. A major complaint of many Alaskans was that the largest, most effective ones were owned and operated by non-Alaskans. In the mid-1920s the commercial fisheries were dominated by Outside capital, cannery labor and fishermen. Although no company or individual could reserve a fishing site from one summer to the next, the relatively permanent pile-driven traps (also known as stationary traps) remained in place, essentially assuring a company of securing its prime fishing site the next season. "All efforts to have them forbidden (in Alaska) have thus far met with defeat, by some insidious method of opposition on the part of the packers that has proven too powerful to overcome," wrote Howard Kutchin in his 1901 report of the salmon fisheries of Alaska. "The tenacious and successful fight for their retention is the more remarkable in view of the fact that they are by no means in general use, and are admittedly not essential to successful fishing operations except in one locality. In Cook Inlet, I'm free to acknowledge, the local conditions make them a necessity, and it is probably true that their disuse there would result in shutting down the canneries." Kutchin wrote those words less than two decades *after* the introduction of fish traps in Alaskan waters and about 57 years *before* the traps were banned.

Several disadvantages existed in the trap fishery. One was that non-targeted species such as porpoise, seals, and beluga were caught

Fidalgo Island Packing Company, in Port Graham, was bustling in the early 1930s, as seen here. *Smith Family Historic Photograph Collection, PM-2005-20-89, Pratt Museum*

During a low tide in the 1950s, men work on a hand trap on a Kenai Peninsula beach. *Mike Steik Historic Photograph Collection, PM-2005-5-7, Pratt Museum*

and drowned accidentally. Over time, however, trap efficiency improved and incidental catches diminished. Also, if the fencing remained in place, traps continued to fish. Occasionally surplus salmon were released but, if not, then they and other animals died a wasteful death.

Elsa Pedersen, who lived in Bear Cove in the 1940s, wrote about her neighbor's harrowing experience.

WHAT A CATCH!

It was autumn in the mid-to-late 1940s when Harry Leonardt boated from his home in Bear Cove to Seldovia to obtain his winter's supply of groceries. On the return, with his skiff heavily laden with food and gear, Harry's outboard engine died. No amount of tinkering could fix it and soon he was drifting northwestward across the mouth of Kachemak Bay toward the wide, uninviting waters of Cook Inlet. Near dusk, the skiff floated alongside the Bluff Point fish trap. Although the fencing and connecting planks had been removed for the winter, rows of bare poles remained firmly planted in the substrate. Luckily, Harry snagged the outermost pole, tied the skiff to it then shimmied to the very top and lashed himself on. Eventually the skiff drifted away. Although his body remained dry, his feet were soaked during every high tide. Slowly, they froze. Through two agonizing days and nights, Harry hung on the pole. Finally, a boatload of searchers pulled up to the pilings. They didn't see Harry, tied as he was like a bundle of rags, until he made a noise to attract their attention. The tough old fox farmer survived but his salt-soaked feet swelled and his toes split open every winter. Harry was lame and in pain for the rest of his life.

Many Alaskans believed that statehood would end the use of the controversial traps and strengthen the opportunity for Alaskans to regulate the fishery. And it did. In 1959 Alaska became the forty-ninth state. Within a year, salmon traps were legislatively banned. Yet even before traps were prohibited, residents had been pioneering other techniques which allowed them to successfully fish salmon in the turbid, tide-powered waters of Cook Inlet and Kachemak Bay.

Today, most commercial salmon fishermen who homeport in Kachemak Bay fish far beyond local waters. The fishery is highly regulated—to the pleasure of some, the displeasure of others. Regardless, the commercial salmon fishery has been an important occupation for Kachemak residents for over a century; with judicious management and habitat protection, hopefully it will remain so for another century.

EXPLORING THE COUNTRY, BUILDING COMMUNITIES

Exploration of the south shore occurred long before that of the north shore. Along the south coast Native peoples and Russian, British and American explorers found deep water for safe anchorage, accessible beaches, salmon-filled streams, seabird rookeries and other amenities which attracted settlement. In contrast, those exploring the north coast found a relatively smooth coastline with mudflats extending far offshore. No embayments provided shelter for boats and large dangerous glacial erratics dotted the flats. In the early 1900s, visitors to the north shore traveled primarily on foot or horseback through unforested country.

Moose populated the meadows as did porcupines and rabbits, black and brown bears and coyotes. Caribou were abundant at one time. The Anchor River, its tributaries and the creeks and rivers meandering across the Fox River Flats supported strong fish runs 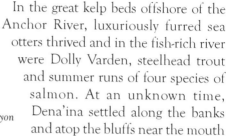 and, on the grassy flats among the waterways, waterfowl and shorebirds fed and nested.

In the great kelp beds offshore of the Anchor River, luxuriously furred sea otters thrived and in the fish-rich river were Dolly Varden, steelhead trout and summer runs of four species of salmon. At an unknown time, Dena'ina settled along the banks and atop the bluffs near the mouth of the river. They called their settlement *Q'es Nalchin* or *Q'es Nasten*, according to Dena'ina elder Peter Kalifornsky. Recent language studies by James Kari provide another name for the Anchor Point site, *K'kaq*, which is translated as "river mouth."

Sea Otter. *Drawing by Gary Lyon*

In the 1800s, Russian fur traders frequented the area, especially with their crews of Native hunters from the Aleutian Islands, the Alaska Peninsula and the Kodiak archipelago. The Russian place name Laida is retained in the contemporary names of Laida Slough and Laida Spit.

Russian clergy, from the Kenai parish, visited outlying settlements on the Peninsula and helped build the Russian Orthodox churches in Seldovia, shown here, and in English Bay. The unpainted tower on the Seldovia church indicates that the photograph was taken in the early 1900s. *Courtesy of Resurrection Bay Historical Society, Seward*

112

No church was built in Laida/Anchor Point although itinerant priests provided services as they traveled through the small settlement. In June 1893, Aleksandr Iaroshevich from the Kenai Mission visited Laida to hold Divine Liturgy. He was greeted by a 75-year-old, strong, vigorous man and observed that 20 people "temporarily" lived in the village along with two shamans. One Laida resident was "Old Iakovlev." Was this the Russian/Dena'ina man who later lived on the south shore of Kachemak Bay and for whom Jakolof Bay was named?

Iaroshevich also held services for the Kennedy family who lived at a place he called Kachemak. (At that time, the huddle of buildings on the tip of the Homer Spit was called Station Coal Point. Whether the Kennedy family lived there, at the base of the Spit, or elsewhere remains unknown.)

Daniel Kennedy, who had left Ireland about 1843 for a life at sea, eventually worked his way to Sitka, Alaska. In 1878, he married Catherine Kvasnikoff, the daughter of a Russian missionary. Later, they moved to Juneau and then in 1892, they and their five sons moved to Kachemak Bay to work a coal claim. When the claim failed to produce within the year, the Kennedy family returned to Juneau. This is a very early reference to a specific family living in Kachemak and to an Orthodox priest conducting services there.

This hand-hewn log house, photographed in 1905, was built in Anchor Point by the Granroos family from Finland, probably in the late 1800s or early 1900s. Inez and Larry Clendenen purchased it in 1947 and recalled that the house was very warm, as the ceiling was insulated with moss and rabbit skins. The structure burned down in 1948. *Adam Widenius Historic Photograph Collection, PM 1994-68-9, Pratt Museum*

Trekking Toward the Gold Fields

In 1898 a group of intrepid gold seekers sailed from King's County, New York, around Tierra del Fuego, up the West Coast of the Americas and into Cook Inlet. Ice forced them to sail into Kachemak Bay where they disembarked and bivouacked near McNeil Canyon on the north shore. On November 10 they wrote and signed a company charter, now preserved in the Pratt Museum. Shortly thereafter, they stuffed their belongings into wheelbarrows and packs and trekked up the Fox River Flats into the heart of the Peninsula. On the southwest shore of Skilak Lake, they hastily built cabins and survived their first and, for most, only winter in Alaska. The next spring, discouraged by hardships, sickness and squabbling, they built rafts and boated down the Kenai River. Most left Alaska. Descendants of the others still live in the Kenai-Soldotna area. King County Creek, flowing into Skilak Lake, was named for this hardscrabble group.

Old-timer, Jay Bibby, right front, talks with Virgo Anderson, Don Ingalls and Fred Anderson about 1939 or 1940. The Anderson brothers moved to Homer in 1924 as young boys, Ingalls taught school near Homer in the late 1930s and Bibby raised cattle near Fox Creek in the 1920s. *Don and Haleen Ingalls Historic Photograph Collection, PM-1977-19-8, Pratt Museum*

The first white settlers on the north shore probably arrived with the mining enterprises, felt the lure of the land and settled in. Little is known of these earliest pioneers. Their stories are revealed in an occasional decaying cabin, an isolated grave marker, place names, a photograph and an occasional trail made as they followed wildlife or visited a distant neighbor. As in the American West, these self-sufficient, single men depended upon the natural resources and their own resourcefulness to sustain themselves. They hunted moose, bear, mountain goat, porcupine, birds and other game, in and out of season, harvested invertebrates and gathered coal to cook their meals and heat their cabins. Would-be seafarers built or purchased boats and fished for herring, salmon, halibut, crab, shrimp and other seafood.

Some pioneers harvested wild edible plants, especially berries, and tilled the soil to plant foods such as broccoli, cabbage, carrots, peas, leafy greens, rhubarb and potatoes—all of which thrive in this cool northern climate. Others experimented with growing grains for livestock they purchased and had shipped from the West Coast at great expense.

<hr />

How Others Saw
Kachemak Country

As men and women slowly settled the north shore, government agents came to assess the agricultural potential of the virgin land. Most visited Kachemak Country for just days or weeks, usually in summer when lush native plants and abundant animal life promised rich harvests. Few visited in winter so they didn't see the dark distances between cabins, the long hours spent collecting and hauling coal, the unending catching and processing of game and the hours spent walking or riding a horse to visit a neighbor miles away. The agents also missed the uniqueness of winter. Even though on the December solstice places on Kachemak Bay receive less than six hours of actual sunlight, ambient light suffuses the land for almost an hour before sunrise and an hour after sunset. Summer visitors also missed the other luminous lights of winter: occasional auroras flaming in night skies, bioluminescence glowing in the cold dark waters and Coleman lanterns spreading their warm glow out cabin windows.

Reports of these government employees provide interesting insights and information, usually accurate, about activities around Kachemak Bay. Some agents visited English Bay, Port Graham and Seldovia in addition to the north shore.

Horses graze on natural pasture on the Homer Spit in 1901. Telephone or telegraph poles, which parallel the railroad bed, may have connected Homer to the mine camp near Bidarka Creek. *U.S. Department of Agriculture, Annual Report of the Office of Experiment Stations, June 30, 1901*

W. A. LANGILLE

In 1904, W.A. Langille, with the U.S. Department of Agriculture, assessed the Kenai Peninsula for consideration as a forest reserve. While visiting that October to December, he noted that Anchor Point had a few Native and 8 to 10 white residents, Homer was abandoned (except for the caretaker) and Seldovia had 75 to 80 Native and 15 white residents. Most Natives lived by hunting and fishing; most whites by trading and prospecting. A few bachelors farmed at the head of Kachemak Bay; otherwise, agricultural development was minimal. Langille observed that with its good, loamy soil much of the Kenai Peninsula would be an important farming and grazing region. He noted that horses and cattle could nearly maintain themselves on the nutritious salt grass growing on the Homer Spit where the snow was swept clean by the wind nearly all winter. (The Spit, however, lacked fresh water and livestock often wandered off to find it.)

Langille also noted that the Kenai Peninsula was home of the largest moose and some of the largest and fiercest bears in the world. Residents and increasing numbers of trophy hunters stalked these majestic animals. (Although Natives told him that moose had arrived on the Peninsula around 1880, bones excavated in archaeological sites indicate that moose inhabited the region centuries earlier. Possibly they had abandoned the Kenai Lowland then returned at a later time.) Langille also noted that by 1904 the immense herds of caribou which had roamed the Lowland were nearly extinct. Market hunters, in particular, had almost exterminated them to feed the miners crowding the gold camps at Sunrise and Hope.

Impressed with the land and wildlife, Langille recommended not only the creation of a Kenai Forest Reserve which would include the north shore of Kachemak Bay, but also of game preserves for Dall sheep, moose and the remnant caribou herds. Today, the Kenai Peninsula Wildlife Refuge contains much of the land he recommended for preservation, except for coastal lands of the north shore.

When Charles C. Georgeson, a special agent for the agricultural experimental stations in Alaska, and Langille investigated the north shore in 1901 and 1904, respectively, few if any people lived on the benchland at the base of the Spit. About 1913 Delphina Woodard (also Woodward) moved to the benchland, one of the first individuals to do so. Not long afterwards, other pioneers were building their homes several miles to the east; an area which became known as Miller's Landing (today Millers Landing) for Charlie Miller who had settled there by 1915. Some of his first neighbors were the Deitz, Nielsen, Palmer and Graham families.

DELPHINA WOODARD
HOMER PIONEER

Delphina Woodard was born in Maine in 1874 and arrived in Homer about 1913, possibly by way of Anchor Point. She was among the earliest settlers of the second community of Homer. Contemporary Homerites recall hearing that her husband, James, drowned while boating between Homer and Seldovia.

Little is known of this quiet, hard-working woman who operated a small-scale dairy farm for several decades. She undoubtedly sold dairy products to resident bachelors and families. She also raised foxes in partnership with Henry Ohlsen.

Delphina Woodard, left, and her partner, most likely Henry Ohlsen, were photographed between 1920 and 1927, probably on her dairy cattle farm in Homer. *Thomas V. (Ted) Palmer Historic Photograph Collection, PM-1998-25-21, Pratt Museum*

Woodard's homesite was located alongside a creeklet near the present junction of the Sterling Highway and Pioneer Avenue. The 161 acres she claimed stretched between the sea bluff and the inland bluff and included much of what today is called "Old Town." Like many pioneers, Woodard lived on her homestead for years before she officially filed for the land. (Around World War I there was a flurry of filing, possibly because more people were moving into the region.)

Woodard died from lung cancer on August 7, 1936, in Seward and was buried there. Henry Ohlsen, the administrator of her estate, sold 158 of her 161 acres at a public auction in Homer. (Did he retain the other three for himself? A small log cabin on Ohlson Lane has been identified as his house.)

W.A. and M.A. Berry purchased Woodard's land for $2,050 then constructed a general mercantile store on what is today the corner of Main and Bunnell. Over the years numerous people owned the store and, with each new owner, the name usually changed. In 2007, the beautifully restored structure contained rental rooms, several small businesses and the Bunnell Street Arts Center.

Woodard Creek, which parallels Bartlett Street and which flowed through her farm, keeps Delphina Woodard's name alive.

There is considerable confusion regarding the spelling of several pioneers' names. Even data on the U.S. Census records is inconsistent. Does the table below, indicate one or two women with the surname Woodard? The birth place and year suggest one. If so, was her name May, or Delfina or Delphina as it's also spelled? Were there one, two or three men named Henry Ohlsen? The birth years imply two but even then, some people were unsure of their age and birth year. The confusion accounts for the various spellings of several Homer place names.

U.S. Census Data	1910	1920	Notes
Anchor Point residents			
May Woodard	Yes	—	Born Maine, 1874
Jas. Woodard	Yes	—	—
Henry Oleson	Yes	—	Born Sweden, 1872
Henry Ohlson	Yes	—	Born Sweden, 1869
Homer residents			
Delfina Woodard	—	Yes	Born Maine, 1874
Henry Ohlsen	—	Yes	Born Sweden, ?

A few Native families still lived in isolated localities such as Bear Cove in the early 1900s. *Steve Zawistowski Collection. Collection of the author*

HUGH BENNETT

Hugh Bennett, with the Department of Agriculture, visited Kachemak Country in 1916. Most people lived in Port Graham, English Bay and Seldovia where their children could attend school, families could attend church and work could be found. Bennett also noted that the 200 or so residents of Seldovia were mostly Natives and descendants of early Russian settlers.

Seasonal employment sustained many residents then as now. Many worked fish traps or toiled in the canneries at Seldovia, Port Graham, Kasilof and Kenai. (The village of Port Graham was founded about 1897 by people from coastal settlements in Prince William Sound and on the Gulf of Alaska. Because it was on deep water, Port Graham became a center for freighting in the early 1900s yet it was the construction of the Fidalgo Island Packing Company cannery about 1911 that provided decades of seasonal employment.) Bennett noted that 3,872 persons, including 728 Natives, were employed in the fisheries in 1915. He also mentioned that a few residents raised and sold beef to the canneries.

Hunting moose, brown and black bears, mountain goats and Dall sheep and trapping foxes, marten, muskrat, mink, weasel and lynx for their hides provided seasonal income. With the demise of the caribou population, Peninsula residents and market hunters killed and sold so many moose to the canneries that the Secretary of Agriculture issued an order, in September 1916, temporarily prohibiting the sale of moose meat on the Peninsula. A beluga hunting business on the west shore of Cook Inlet occurred during 1916. Initiated by Kenai hunters, the whales were killed for their oil and also for their hides from which shoe leather, shoe laces and gloves were made. (The beluga fishery occurred again in 1919 and possibly in 1920 and 1922.)

F. (FEATHERSTONE) W. WILLIAMSON

The first general land surveys from Anchor Point eastward toward the head of Kachemak Bay and south to the base of the Homer Spit were conducted in 1917 and 1918 by F. W. Williamson and his assistants. As the men hiked the rugged terrain, they mapped the topography and recorded some place names and a few residents' names. They also indicated the locations of a salmon fish trap near Diamond Creek and several coal mining sites.

On the 1918 survey map, Williamson identified three residents south of the Anchor Point River. Near a small ditch was Tom Rapetta's house and garden (A) and farther south was Newton Shular's place (B). Educated as a mining engineer, Shular purchased the buildings of the defunct Anchor Point Mining Company which had mined for placer gold. He was there not to pan for gold but to raise foxes. He had about 10 fox pens, 50 feet by 100 feet each, for his 50 or so foxes. A trail led from Shular's home to the lengthy mining ditch which

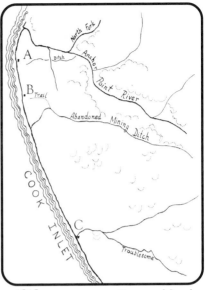

1918 survey map. *Bureau of Land Management. Map redrawn by Kay VanDervoort*

had been hand dug in the mid-1890s. Farther south on the map was the house of William Ritter (C) built alongside the mouth of Troublesome Creek. A prospector and miner, Ritter died from apoplexy and was buried by the survey crew.

Place names on that first survey include Laida Creek and Slough, the Anchor Point River, North Fork Anchor Point River and Troublesome Creek. The rolling and level land, especially atop the sea bluff around Anchor Point, was described as primarily moss and tundra.

Marked on the 1917 survey map showing Homer were two gardens, Delphina Woodard's house, Denny's house, an unidentified cabin and Mud Lake Bed, today Beluga Slough. A trail, probably atop the old railroad grade, connected the houses then snaked up the bluff into the high country toward Diamond Creek, Twitter Creek and Ohlson Mountain. Unfortunately,

Williamson's notes don't indicate whether the features were named by him, his crew or residents. Several cabins were indicated at the mouth of Fritz Creek but those of people living near Millers Landing were not shown. The Homer benchland was characterized by marshy areas alongside areas of naturally drained land, all covered with a heavy growth of redtop grass interspersed with dense alders and willows and clumps of young spruce and birch.

BUILDING COMMUNITIES

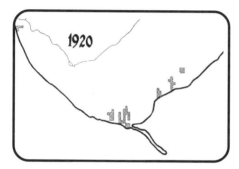

Lands designated on a 1920 schematic show settlement from Anchor Point, upper left, to Homer and eastward to Millers Landing. *Johnson and Coffman*

As the 1920s unfolded, the population of Homer grew. Slowly a community developed. In 1924, Gustav and Maren Anderson moved from Seldovia to Homer, established a homestead and settled in to raise their children, Virgo, Fred and Vega. Nels Olaf Svedlund and his son, Garen, homesteaded next to the Andersons and the families built their homes about the same time, trading knowledge and skills. Descendants of the Andersons and other early families still live in the area.

With families settling at Anchor Point, Homer, Millers Landing and in between, transportation, communication, schooling and other necessities became important. On the Homer benchland, the first school was built on the Nielsen homestead in 1919, the first telephone wires were strung in the early 1920s and the first road was constructed in 1925. It extended eastward and westward from Millers Landing. Beaches of the north shore served as roads and trips were planned around the tides.

Oris "Pa" Russell. *Willam Wakeland Historic Photograph Collection, PM-1982-77-33, Pratt Museum*

Between 1901 and about 1920, there were few reasons for residents to visit the deserted coal town on the Homer Spit especially since walking or riding a horse along the railroad bed or rowing a boat took considerable time. The railroad engines, cars, rails and other equipment were removed between 1913 and 1915 by a West Coast salvage company. Around 1920, fishing boats owned by local canneries began plying Kachemak Bay. Ten years later privately owned fishing boats came into common use.

Ted Palmer. *Chris Russ, permission of the Homer News, Homer, Alaska*

Ted Palmer, who lived near Homer in the 1920s, revisited the area in 1998 at the age of 92, donated a collection of photographs to the Pratt Museum and told many interesting stories about life on the north shore. Ted was 14 years old when he, his brother and his parents, Isabella and John Palmer, a blacksmith, moved into a previously occupied log cabin in the wilderness near Bear Creek in 1920. The family left in 1927 after Mr. Palmer died. Palmer Creek, which drains Bear Canyon, acknowledges them. (In 2000, the cabin the Palmers occupied was moved. The Nordby cabin, as many contemporary residents call it, now functions as the living room and kitchen of a two story house on Nordby Avenue.)

The 1920s was also the period of Prohibition. The 18th

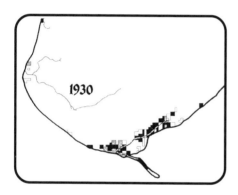

Growth prior to 1930 continued in Homer and expanded along the road to the east. Numerous commercial businesses were established during the 1930s. *Johnson and Coffman*

Amendment, ratified in January 1919, and the Volstead Act, passed in October of the same year, prohibited the manufacture, sale, transportation and export and import of alcoholic beverages in the United States and its territories, including Alaska.

Steve Zawistowski, who came to Kachemak Country in 1930, said in a Kachemak Bay Broadcasting radio program, that a still was secluded in almost every embayment along the south shore, including Charlie Dennison's "large distillery in Aurora Lagoon." Larry and Inez Clendenen, who purchased the Granroos property in Anchor Point in 1947, discovered several stills where the former owners had made whiskey to sell. Because prohibition officers or "pro-highs" as Zawistowski called them, seldom visited Kachemak Country, bootleggers were relatively free to develop and market their moonshine. When Prohibition was repealed in 1933,

Zawistowski laughingly lamented that many locals lost their income.

Today, residents make raspberry cordial, potato vodka and rhubarb, fireweed and dandelion wines from domestic or wild plants.

People seeking relief from the Great Depression in the contiguous United States came to Alaska to participate in a land program in the Matanuska Valley, north of Anchorage, in the mid-1930s. A handful found their way to Kachemak Country and homesteaded atop the second benchland. In 1935, Homer was described in the Alaska Directory as having a population of 127 with some Native residents, a post office, a bank and two schools—one at Homer and one at Kachemak Bay (Millers Landing). Cattle raising, fox farming and fishing were listed as the main industries while natural resources included "gold, copper, coal & natural gas." The mention of gold probably referred to the placer mining near Anchor Point; the reference to copper and a bank is perplexing.

Considerable commercial development occurred in the 1930s. Delphina Woodard died in 1936 and some of the first commercial businesses were built on her homestead. The original dock, built on the Spit in 1899 and later destroyed by ice, was rebuilt in 1938 by members of the Homer Civic League. (The dock was destroyed and reconstructed several more times.) With a deepwater dock, residents no longer needed to boat to Seldovia to obtain their annual supplies.

Henry Chamberlain, Joe Wallace and George Kirkpatrick chat alongside the well-stocked shelves of Chamberlain and Watson's mercantile store in 1947. *William Wakeland Historic Photograph Collection, PM-1982-77-37, Pratt Museum*

A 1946 photograph shows some of the oldest commercial buildings still in use in 2007: left to right, the community hall (relocated to Pioneer Avenue), the Homer Café and Club (now Duggan's Waterfront Pub), and Berry's mercantile store (now Bunnell Street Arts Center.) The store had numerous owners and names: Berry's, Bunnell's, Chamberlain and Watson's, Bishop's, and the Inlet Trading Post. *Steve McCutcheon Collection, Anchorage Museum*

Natalie Hewlett photograph, Office of History and Archaeology, Anchorage

William and Agnes Putnam built this residence on Main Street in the late 1930s. The upper level was their home; the lower provided office space for businesses such as Cook Inlet Flying Service and Woodley Airlines which became Pacific Northern Airlines. In the late 1940s, Arthur and Natalie Hewlett purchased the house and, in 1950, opened the first

Bank of Homer. He managed it. Elmer Rasmuson took control of the bank in 1954 and later merged it into the National Bank of Alaska with A. R. "Russ" Cronin as its first manager. The Putnam/Hewlett house was torn down in the 1990s.

> If you want a beautiful place to live, a wonderful place, you ought to go to Homer. There's the homesteading country, rolling hills, little clumps of spruce trees here and there, the grass is seven feet tall and moose all over; that's the perfect place."
>
> A 1939 territorial surveyor's impression as told to Paul Banks

Paul Banks, who stands alongside his original log cabin in 1986, left Anchorage in 1941 to homestead in the hills above Homer. Unable to make a living from the land, he worked at many occupations through the years. Eventually, he moved into Homer and became the beloved accordion-playing, song-writing custodian at East Homer Elementary School. Seven years before his death in 1988, the school was renamed in his honor.

Had Paul Banks heard a more accurate description of the challenges and vagaries of homesteading, he might never have pursued that way of life. To be more

Dorothy Cline Historic Photograph Collection, PM-2006-7-7, Pratt Museum

accurate, the surveyor's description should have read: If you want a beautiful place to live, a wonderful place, you ought to go to Homer; however, do not go there to homestead. Although it looks like prime homesteading and ranching country with rolling hills, grass that grows seven feet tall and many moose, it's not the ideal place for homesteading. Cold, damp soils are insulated by thick layers of

127

vegetation which decay slowly, rain often falls during the harvest season and snow can last long into spring. If one successfully raises a good crop or livestock to sell, inadequate, costly transportation and distant buyers cause marketing to be most challenging.

Only a few people made a living from the land. Like Banks, most combined seasonal jobs such as logging, fishing, boat building, longshoring, surveying, and road construction and maintenance with tending their land and animals. Some opened retail businesses as demands from the growing population increased.

"You did whatever Alaskans did in those days—whatever came along," said Helen March, an Alaskan-born woman who retired to Homer in 1977 and then moved to Anchorage in the 1990s.

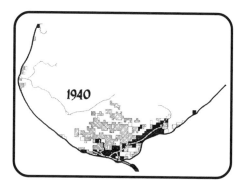

Growth during the 1930s spread into the Homer hills and eastward. Although it abated in the first half of the 1940s, it increased after World War II. *Johnson and Coffman*

During the 1940s, basic services and facilities continued to be developed. Homesteading, World War II, revived interest in coal mining, construction of a permanent road to the Spit and construction of the Sterling Highway galvanized the economy.

The tiny settlement of Anchor Point experienced an influx of people from 1943 to 1949 after Ruth Kyllonen started a mission for a Christian community. Within a few years, Louvie (Vi) and Sherman Chapman, Alice and Leo Eason and the Clark Peterson family, among others, joined Kyllonen and her son, Buzz. By 1949 the community established its first post office and first territorial school so residents no longer needed to travel to Homer as often.

Developing
The North Shore

Period	Entries		Patented		Major Events
Up to 1920	17	2,305 acres	8	1,110 acres	World War I
1921–1930	61	7,325 acres	36	4,082 acres	Prohibition, Dust Bowl
1931–1940	165	21,191 acres	65	7,984 acres	Dust Bowl
1941–1945	86	11,031 acres	24	2,621 acres	World War II
1946–1950	172	21,543 acres	98	12,201 acres	Post-World War
1951–1955	237	29,803 acres	19	2,365 acres	Cold War

Table showing homesteading activities from the early 1900s to 1955. Despite the glowing descriptions of the agricultural potential of the region, agriculture, as a viable economy, never succeeded. *Johnson and Coffman*

Try Again was an often photographed derelict boat on the Homer Spit. Its name symbolized the attitude of many residents who approached the vagaries of life with determination and an attitude that allowed them to transition from one job to another. *Courtesy of Debbie Smith*

World War II impacted Kachemak residents in numerous ways. Residents stockpiled food, water and supplies, hung blackout curtains, watched for submarines and, at the request of the government, compiled a list of armaments in each household. A major benefit of the war period was the construction of the Homer airstrip in 1941 which served as a refueling stop for military planes en route to Kodiak and the Aleutian Islands. (Although originally about 8,000 feet long, the runway was shortened later.) Having regularly scheduled transportation to Kodiak allowed gardeners to ship produce to the troops stationed there. World War II also stimulated a renewed interest in the mining of chromite, especially at Red Mountain near Seldovia, and coal near Homer.

Evan Jones has been called the father of the coal industry in Alaska. Born in Wales in 1880, he immigrated to Alaska and developed coal mines north of Anchorage. About 1943 he moved to Homer where, with an absentee partner, he started the Homer Coal Company and reopened the old mines. Although he sought to sell coal to the military, he didn't succeed. Jones died peacefully at his home in Homer in 1950.

Evan Jones, upper photograph, shows an Army sergeant a sample of coal in the Homer mine. The sergeant also visited the Homer Cash Store where Lillian Walli worked behind the counter. *Both: Steve McCutcheon Collection, Anchorage Museum*

Miners, in the 1940s, ride a car along the bluff face to the bluff top where coal was stockpiled. The metal cable from the winch still hung over the bluff in 2005. *Enoch Nordby Historic Photograph Collection, PM-1998-6-107B, Pratt Museum*

The remains of several coal cars, such as this one, were found in an alder patch near Bidarka Creek and excavated by the author in 1995. The landowner donated them to the Pratt Museum.

Dave Brann, a railroad aficionado and Homer teacher, helped recover them. Several years later his workshop class restored the side-dumping car which is 60-inches long, 36-inches wide and 33-inches high and sits on a 24-inches-wide rail at the museum. The car was probably used in the tunnels in the 1940s and possibly in the open pit mines in the late 1950s.

Prior to 1945, north shore residents accessed the Homer Spit via the old railroad bed or on the road descending the hill south of Lake Street, today an abrupt cliff. In 1945 after waves repeatedly washed out access to the Spit, the Alaska Road Commission constructed a new road through the mud, muck and the middle of what became known as Mud Bay. (About 1985 the lagoon opposite Mud Bay became known as Mariner Park.) Timber for cribbing was cut on the Peterson/China Poot Peninsula (today called the Island Peninsula) and rafted to the Spit. Gravel for the Spit road, other roads and also for the airstrip, was removed from the base of the Spit and from near Munson Point, to the west. The removal of tons of gravel over many years caused and exacerbated erosion that continues into the twenty-first century.

Construction of the Homer Spit road, 1945. *Ralph Soberg photograph. Courtesy of Jackie Pels*

Throughout the decades, Kachemak residents remained, and remain, resourceful when it came to putting food on their tables. In addition to harvesting seafoods and hunting large and small game, they supplemented their diets with wild edibles such as berries, greens and mushrooms. For Joel and Bob Moss who lived in Peterson Bay in the late 1940s and 1950s, Gull Island was like a table set for dining. The brothers would boat to the island, toss all the gull eggs into the sea then return within a few days to harvest fresh eggs. They also collected the nutrient-rich nests at the end of summer to enrich the impoverished soil at their home sites.

HELEN AND MILTON ALM
HOMER RESIDENTS

Helen Alm in her nursing cap and gown, 1934. Milton Alm aboard a fishing boat in the late 1940s. *Left: Courtesy of Helen Alm and, right, William Wakeland*

Milton (Milt) and Helen Alm were the quintessential Homer residents: hard-working, relatively self-sufficient, friendly and always willing to help others.

Helen Jacobson, born in Seattle, and Milton Alm, born in Dawson City, Yukon Territory, were married in Seattle in 1935. Milt's father had participated in the Klondike gold rush of 1898 and his mother had lived in Nome when it was a tent city in 1899, so it's not surprising that the north country appealed to him. A month after he and Helen were married, they boarded the S.S. *Yukon* for Alaska. After not finding their golden fortune in Livengood or Fairbanks, they purchased 10 acres, sight unseen, in Homer for $70 an acre. With Marilyn and Barbara, their daughters, they moved to Homer in 1945 where they built a three-story concrete-block-and-log home on lower East Hill Road.

Milt started Homer Automotive with Ben Bellamy and then, several years later, he began commercial fishing. He died unexpectedly in 1967. Helen, who had earned her nursing degree in 1934 in Portland, worked as a professional nurse in Homer until her retirement in 1991. She delivered many babies, nursed many residents back to health and sheltered children and adults who needed a safe haven or a helping hand. Long after her retirement, when Helen reminisced about nursing, she remained professional and never disclosed a patient's name.

Helen died in 2008 in the log home she and Milt built. She left behind a town full of friends and admirers. Alm Lane honors these community-spirited residents.

Kachemak Country is berry-rich. Wild blueberries and raspberries, lowbush and highbush cranberries, currants, salmonberries, crowberries, and watermelon berries along with domestic raspberries, strawberries, gooseberries and others provided, and still provide, fruit for jams, jellies, pies, sauces and drinks.

This small log building has housed Alaska Wild Berry Products for over 60 years. Founded by Ken and Hazel Heath in 1946, the Homer business capitalized upon the abundance and varieties of local berries. *Both: Historic Photograph Collection, Pratt Museum*

The Thorn-Stingley House represents a classic frame house built in Homer. Constructed with locally cut lumber in 1945, it retains many original details in part because it has had only two owners, Francis and Faye Thorn and

134

Richard Stingley. In 2001 the architecturally attractive, well-maintained house was listed on the National Register of Historic Places, the federal government's list of properties worthy of preservation.

As the population of Kachemak Country increased, local, regional and territorial news became important. Prior to the 1940s, news about Kachemak people and communities appeared in newspapers in Sitka, Seward and Seldovia. In 1944 the *Homer Homesteader* was established and the first iteration of the *Homer News* was published in 1950. Later, it was renamed the *Kenai Peninsula Pioneer*.

At the close of the 1940s construction of the road between Seward and Homer began. Residents found seasonal employment with the survey and construction crews and permanent employment with the Alaska Road Commission which opened an office in Homer.

HAWLEY STERLING
ROAD BUILDER

Alaska Highway #1, the Sterling Highway, extends northward from Homer along the bluffs of Cook Inlet then cuts inland to join the Seward Highway east of Cooper Landing.

The route was laid out in 1945 by Hawley Sterling, the assistant chief engineer of the Alaska Road Commission. He died in 1948 and a year later the road was designated the Sterling Highway.

Construction started early in 1949 and by June, segments connected Seward to Kasilof, Kasilof to Clam Gulch and Anchor Point to Homer. With the completion of the Clam Gulch-Anchor Point segment in 1950, the road was finished but not necessarily easy to drive. *Hawley W. Sterling Historic Photograph Collection, PM-2006-35-3, Pratt Museum*

Cowboys enjoy lunch on the Fox River Flats, 1964. Left to right, front row: Atz Kilcher, Milton Lewis, Elvin Lewis, and Matt Mattox; back row, Joe Tietjen, Tom Tietjen, Charles Rainwater; horses are Senator, Roanie and Cha-cha. *Soil Conservation Service Historic Photograph Collection, PM-1987-27-27, Pratt Museum*

Northeastward from Homer, the "wild west" existed in a small population of men who resided in the Fox River valley and raised cattle. Among the earliest were Alfred Clark, Jay Bibby and a Scotsman named Thoroughgood. In the 1940s and 1950s, others moved into the lowland country including Hazel and Oris Russell, Alvia "Matt" Mattox and Carl Heileman. In 1952, C.W. Rainwater and C.J. Kunz homesteaded atop the benchlands and filed for a grazing lease in the valley. To accommodate others wanting to run their cattle on the flats, the Fox River Cattlemen's Association was formed by Rainwater, Kunz, Mattox and Yule Kilcher who had purchased Clark's place and who homesteaded near McNeil Canyon in the late 1940s.

The cattle roamed free on the flats, growing well on the summer grasslands which the association leased annually. Every fall the cowboys rounded up the cattle then herded them along the beach to winter on farm land near Homer. In spring, the cattle were driven back to the flats. For many years, people could purchase grass-fed beef and have it processed locally.

Today, cowboys still ride the flats and round up and brand cattle. Fences, however, now restrict their freedom somewhat and much wintering land near Homer has been subdivided.

The remoteness and difficult access made the Fox River Flats a challenging and lonely place to live, but it was open, relatively unsettled land rich in freedom and opportunity for those willing to work hard and, often, work alone. Corky Mattox Wieber lived with her father, Matt Mattox, near Fox Creek when she was in her 40s. "At that time, it was very definitely a man's country," she recalled when visiting Homer in 2003. "Many women came only because their husbands came. It was very lonesome for a woman. I remember wanting to cry every time I thought about California but I got over it and loved it."

As the second half of the twentieth century began, Homer had two general stores, a drug store, several groceries, two hotels, one motel, automotive garages, crab and fish canneries, a hospital with one doctor, a telephone system, a post office and numerous churches. Many community organizations were active such as the

Clem Tillion and William "Bill" Wakeland processed their winter's supply of moose and geese on the floor of Bill's home in Seldovia. *William Wakeland Historic Photograph Collection, PM-1982-77-58, Pratt Museum*

The expanding road system allowed for improved access and stimulated settlement on the Kenai Peninsula. *Johnson and Coffman*

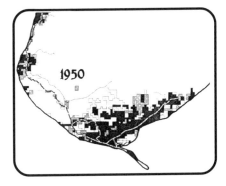

137

American Legion, the Chamber of Commerce, the Elks Club and the Homer Volunteer Fire Department and Auxiliary.

As Homer grew, north shore residents conducted a forward-thinking self-assessment utilizing an established program, the Citizens Study Group, developed and used Outside. Weekly meetings were held during the winter of 1952 to discuss such topics as sidewalks, landscaping, zoning and governance—issues still discussed. Also considered was whether or not to change the name of the town; after all, who really wanted a town named after a known swindler? Apparently, Homerites did!

Residents were now linked by sea, air and road to the rest of the Kenai Peninsula and beyond. With those connections, the cultural and physical landscape changed inevitably and irrevocably. In Homer, the Alaska Road Commission established and operated a maintenance and construction facility, the Civil Aeronautics Administration maintained the airstrip, and the Public Utilities District (PUD), the first political subdivision, replaced the Homer Civic League. PUD members managed the dock, the harbor facilities and the hospital while Homer Electric Association powered up to serve 56 members in the immediate area. (At the end of 2007, HEA served over 20,000 customers spread across 3,000 square miles.)

The majority of salmon processing plants still operated in Seldovia but, otherwise, Homer had replaced that community as the commercial, economic and social center in lower Cook Inlet. It would take the world's second largest earthquake and the community-altering aftereffects before Homer usurped Seldovia as the principal seafood processing center.

Gardening and raising small livestock remained important in the 1950s as they do today. Cool weather crops thrived in the long lingering light of summers. Residents raised bees, meat chickens, laying hens, sheep, goats and dairy and beef cattle for personal use. The high costs of supplemental feed, farming equipment and transportation to markets, even within Alaska, still deterred commercial-sized enterprises. The Lofgren family, who operated a commercially successful chicken ranch on Diamond Ridge, was one of the few who made their living from animal husbandry.

Coal remained the heating fuel of choice. It was available free from the beaches or could be purchased from men such as Whitey

Schenk and Matt Mattox. Jack Gist and Bruno Agostino operated strip mines in 1959 in east Homer and near Bidarka Creek, respectively. Today, coal is still gathered from the beaches and used to heat homes. As fuel costs soar, it will be interesting to see if there will be an increase in the number of coal collectors.

Homer, in 1953, was concentrated on the bluff just above the bay. Today, this area of Homer is known as "Old Town." *Steve McCutcheon Collection, Anchorage Museum*

Two significant events occurred in 1964 which changed the character and face of Kachemak Country. After months of debate, Homerites voted in March to incorporate as the City of Homer. The paperwork was sent to Anchorage for certification. On March 27, the largest earthquake in North America shook Southcentral Alaska. While widespread devastation struck dozens of communities, including Anchorage, someone remembered to sign the papers of incorporation designating Homer as a first-class city. That designation allowed the newly elected city council to apply for federal funds to construct a small boat harbor within the confines of the Spit, an action which forever changed the nature of the Spit and of Kachemak Bay communities.

Downtown Seldovia, in 1954, was concentrated along the waterfront where homes and businesses were connected by the community-built boardwalk. *Steve McCutcheon Collection, Anchorage Museum*

UNSETTLING
THE 1964 EARTHQUAKE

Nineteen sixty-four was a pivotal year in the history of Southcentral Alaska. The largest earthquake in North America and the second largest recorded in the world occurred on March 27. It had a moment magnitude of 9.2. (The greatest earthquake ever recorded prior to 2007 occurred in Chile in 1960 and had a magnitude of 9.5.)

Centered in Prince William Sound, about 150 air miles northeast of Kachemak Bay, the 1964 earthquake and tsunamis caused widespread devastation throughout Southcentral Alaska and along the coasts of Canada, Oregon, California and Hawaii.

A combination of earth movement, land subsidence and tsunamis destroyed the Native villages of Chenega and Tatitlik, much of the City of Valdez, the tiny community of Portage, the waterfronts of Seward and Kodiak and commercial and residential areas of Anchorage. Kenai, Whittier, Hope, Homer and other communities experienced varying degrees of damage. The quake killed 15 people; the tsunamis 110. No lives were lost in Kachemak Country during the almost five interminable minutes of ground movement on that Good Friday.

Throughout Southcentral Alaska some land was uplifted, some sank. In Kachemak Bay the unconsolidated sediments deposited in the last 10,000 years slumped and subsided, some by as much as eight feet. Many residents were unaware that the land had sunk. Traditionally, seaside structures had been built atop wooden pilings to elevate them above the high tides. Days after the quake, residents in Halibut Cove and Seldovia, in particular, watched in disbelief as the tides rose, flooded their walkways and seeped or rushed into buildings.

In homes and businesses, prolonged and severe earth movement caused objects to crash and break, people to stagger around and buildings to crack. Fissures snaked across roads, boats tore loose from their moorings and animals raced around in panic.

Along the coast, low-lying sandspits, meadows and estuaries were inundated with salt water. Over the years, excessive salt killed the trees. Remnant ghost forests with dead, whitened trunks and exposed roots still stand along the south shore, graphic reminders of the dynamic nature of this place.

SELDOVIA

Seldovia was seriously affected by the earthquake. Prior to that event, at least five processors employed about 200 people to pack salmon, crab and shrimp. Fishing and fish-related businesses had formed the economic foundation of the picturesque seaside town for decades. Stretching along the waterfront was the boardwalk which residents had built in the late 1920s and then widened in 1931 to function as a roadway for small vehicles. The boardwalk represented not only the independent spirit but also the physical allure and identity which many people perceived to be the essence of Seldovia. The boardwalk was not severely damaged by the earthquake itself, but the high tides of summer and fall washed over it revealing that it and the entire waterfront had subsided.

Many structures were repeatedly flooded by high tides. Residents coped as best they could under the physical and emotional uncertainties of the future.

What were residents and businesses to do? Could the boardwalk and associated

Both: Record Group 77, U.S. Army Corps of Engineers

structures be elevated? The Seldovia city council called upon the government to help assess the situation and suggest alternatives for rebuilding. Contentious debates occurred as various plans were proposed. Seldovians were

pitted one against another as the future of their community was determined. Ultimately the city council voted to approve Urban Renewal and, with it, Seldovia was transmogrified. Razed were Cap's Hill in downtown and most of the boardwalk. Moved was the old cemetery. Added were new roads and new zoning and building codes. On the heels of such radical change nearly 20 families and nine businesses including all but one seafood processor, left Seldovia. In a community with a population of about 450, that loss was devastating.

The long-term economic loss and emotional upheaval impacted the community severely. The earthquake destroyed Seldovia's prominence as the commercial hub of lower Cook Inlet when the canneries were demolished during Urban Renewal. Some Seldovians felt that the rebuilding of their town inflicted more damage than did the earthquake. Over 40 years later, the mention

143

of Urban Renewal can still generate emotional responses from those who remained in Seldovia and those who left. Today, the resilient residents focus on maintaining the uniqueness and charm that have always characterized Seldovia. A remnant section of the boardwalk remains and reminds us of the unpredictability of living in an environment where earthquakes, volcanic eruptions, tsunamis, landslides, flooding and other natural events occur.

HOMER

Interminable shaking on the north shore lasted about five minutes. Much of the damage to Homer occurred on the Spit which subsided between four and six feet. "Part of the subsidence was tectonic and part—especially at the seaward end—was probably the result of compaction of the unconsolidated gravel. . ." according to a U.S. Geological Survey report. Because the Spit had been higher, structures had not been built atop pilings. When subsequent tides flooded them, owners were forced to demolish, move or jack up their structures. The newly constructed Porpoise Room restaurant, near the harbor, opened the day after the quake and closed the next day with just enough time to schedule 'Grand Opening' and 'Going Out of Business' events.

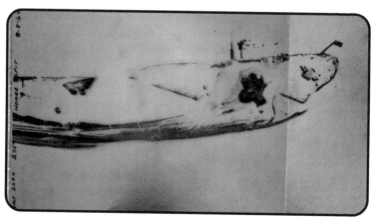

The Homer Spit consisted of approximately 508 acres, most of which were above the highest tides prior to the 1964 earthquake. Five months after the quake, much of the tip of the Spit, above, and about 300 acres were underwater during high tides. *U.S. Bureau of Land Management*

144

Water gushed through the door and windows of the Salty Dawg Saloon. Later the saloon and nearby Salty Pup Café were moved onto higher land and combined into a single unit with several other buildings. *Steve McCutcheon Collection, Anchorage Museum*

Joel Moss, a former surveyor and fisherman, told the author that in one respect the 1964 earthquake was the best thing to happen to the Homer economy because federal funds were made available for the construction of a boat harbor *within* the confines of the Spit. With the infusion of money, the newly incorporated City of Homer found itself immersed in the construction of a modern small boat harbor.

With new facilities, development of the fisheries and fish-related businesses on the Spit accelerated and Homer became the center of commercial fishing and processing on the lower Kenai Peninsula. As commercial, sports and personal use fishing increased along with recreational and commercial boating, so did demands on the Homer Small Boat Harbor. After several expansions, it has become the largest single boat basin in Alaska with 48 acres and 920 boat slips in 2007. Adjacent to, yet outside of the harbor, two docks handle large ocean-going vessels.

Over time stands of spruce killed by salt water, the buildings, even the last stretch of the original Seldovia boardwalk, will disappear, as will the emotional scars. The stories written by those who experienced the catastrophe, however, will survive to remind us of what can happen along the shores of Kachemak Bay.

EPILOGUE

Kachemak Country remains a good place to live—whether on the north or south shore, in town or country, in an expensive home or modest cabin. A strong sense of community and a vibrant spirit characterize Kachemak residents.

Everywhere, winter is a time to reconnect with friends and activities put on hold during the frenzied days of summer: musical and dance performances, art exhibits, museum activities, school and college classes, and the myriad events sponsored by over 50 non-profit organizations in Homer alone. When the weather is cold enough, residents delight in skiing, ice skating, snow machining and other outdoor activities. For many, it is also a time to travel to exotic shores or visit family and friends Outside.

The stunning beauty of the Kachemak triptych remains in winter. Following a snowfall, the entire bay is often touched by an ephemeral beauty and tranquility; sunrises and sunsets brush the skies with a fresh palette—lemon, apricot, peach, pale green, lavender, even deep purple—and lambent light reflects from the often still waters. Along the south shore tiny enclaves of people nestle in the winter shadow of the Kenai Mountains and bask in the prolonged hours of summer sun. Along the north shore, residents bask in winter sunshine and marvel as the summer sun highlights the glaciers and rocky crests of the distant mountains. The Dena'ina people called the Kenai Peninsula *Yaghanen*, the 'good land.' To many of us, that name says it all.

MAPS

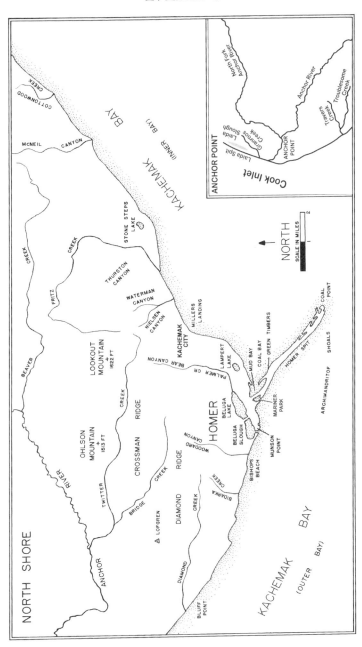

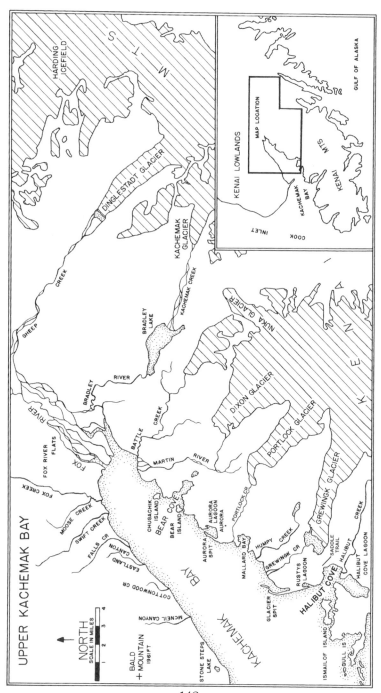

UPPER KACHEMAK BAY

NORTH

SCALE IN MILES

1 2 3 4

BALD
+ MOUNTAIN
1961 FT

HARDING
ICEFIELD

KENAI LOWLANDS

MAP LOCATION

GULF OF ALASKA

KENAI MTS

KACHEMAK
BAY

COOK INLET

DINGLESTADT GLACIER

KACHEMAK GLACIER

SHEEP CREEK

BRADLEY LAKE

KACHEMAK CREEK

NUKA GLACIER

BRADLEY RIVER

DIXON GLACIER

PORTLOOK GLACIER

GREWINGK GLACIER

FOX RIVER FLATS

FOX RIVER

FOX CREEK

MOOSE CREEK

SWIFT CREEK

FALLS CR

BATTLE CREEK

MARTIN RIVER

PORTLOOK CR

EASTLAND CANYON

COTTONWOOD CR

CHUGACHIK ISLAND

BEAR COVE

BEAR COVE ISLAND

AURORA SPIT

AURORA LAGOON

AURORA

MALLARD BAY

HUMPY CREEK

GREWINGK CR

SADDLE TRAIL

HALIBUT CREEK

HALIBUT COVE LAGOON

MCNEIL CANYON

KACHEMAK BAY

GLACIER SPIT

RUSTYS LAGOON

HALIBUT COVE

STONE STEPS LAKE

ISMAILOF ISLAND

GULL IS

148

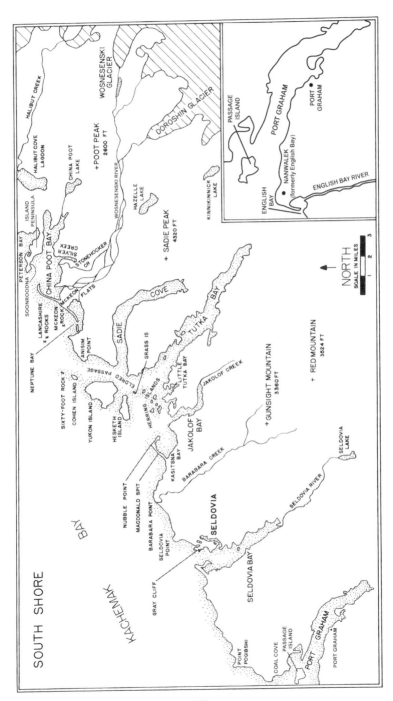

SOUTH SHORE

KACHEMAK BAY

HALIBUT CREEK

WOSNESENSKI GLACIER

DOROSHIN GLACIER

HALIBUT COVE LAGOON

CHINA POOT LAKE

+POOT PEAK 2800 FT

WOSNESENSKI RIVER

HAZELLE LAKE

ISLAND PENINSULA

PETERSON BAY

SILVER CREEK

STONEHOCKER

CHINA POOT BAY

KINNIKINNICK LAKE

+ SADIE PEAK 4320 FT

SOONROODNA

LANCASHIRE

McKEON ROCKS x x ROCKS
McKEON FLATS

NEPTUNE BAY

SADIE COVE

ANISIM POINT

ELDRED PASSAGE

SIXTY-FOOT ROCK

COHEN ISLAND

YUKON ISLAND

HESKETH ISLAND

HERRING ISLANDS

GRASS IS

LITTLE TUTKA BAY

TUTKA BAY

JAKOLOF CREEK

+ GUNSIGHT MOUNTAIN 3380 FT

+ RED MOUNTAIN 3524 FT

JAKOLOF BAY

KASITSNA BAY

BARABARA CREEK

NUBBLE POINT

MACDONALD SPIT

BARABARA POINT

SELDOVIA POINT

SELDOVIA

SELDOVIA RIVER

SELDOVIA LAKE

GRAY CLIFF

SELDOVIA BAY

POINT POGIBSHI

COAL COVE

PASSAGE ISLAND

PORT GRAHAM

PORT GRAHAM

NORTH
SCALE IN MILES
1 2 3

PASSAGE ISLAND

PORT GRAHAM

PORT GRAHAM

ENGLISH BAY

NANWALEK (formerly English Bay)

ENGLISH BAY RIVER

149

SELECT BIBLIOGRAPHY

Alaska Commercial Company Records. 1868-1913, Box 10, Folder 120. *English Bay Station Log Book, May 15, 1883–July 1884.* Archives, University of Alaska Fairbanks, Elmer E. Rasmuson Library, Alaska and Polar Regions Collections, Fairbanks.

Alaska Directory Company, publisher. *Alaska Directory & Gazetteer, 1934-1935.* Seattle and Fairbanks: Alaska Directory Company, 1935.

Bailey, Edgar P. *Introduction of Foxes to Alaskan Islands – History, Effects on Avifauna, and Eradication.* U.S. Fish and Wildlife Service Resource Publication 193, 1993.

Banks, Della Murray. "Homer's Gold Seekers," four chapters. Ketchikan: The Alaska Sportsman, Oct., Nov., Dec., 1945, Jan., 1946.

Barry, Mary J. *A History of Mining on the Kenai Peninsula.* Anchorage: Alaska Northwest Publishing Company, 1976.

Bean, Tarleton. "Notes on Birds Collected During the Summer of 1880 in Alaska and Siberia." *In Proceedings of the United States National Museum, 1882.* U. S. Department of the Interior, 1883.

Becker, George F. "Reconnaissance of the Gold Fields of Southern Alaska with Some Notes of General Geology." Extract from U.S. Geological Survey 18th Annual Report, 1896-97, Part III, 1898.

Bennett, Hugh H. "Report on a Reconnaissance of the Soils, Agriculture, and Other Resources of the Kenai Peninsula Region of Alaska." U.S. Bureau of Soils, 1918.

Bolz, Peter and Hans-Ulrich Sanner. *Native American Art, the Collections of the Ethnological Museum Berlin.* Berlin: Reiter-Druck, 1999.

Bradley, Dwight C., Timothy M. Kusky, Peter J. Haeussler, Susan M. Karl, and D. Thomas Donley. *Geologic Map of the Seldovia Quadrangle, South-central Alaska.* U.S. Geological Survey Open-file Report OF 99-18, 1999.

Cane, Colonel Claude. *Summer and Fall in Western Alaska: The Record of a Trip to Cook's Inlet After Big Game.* London: Horace Cox, 1903.

Cline, Dorothy R., editor. *The Paul Banks Songbook.* Homer: The Homer Foundation, 2001.

Cole, Terrence and Elmer E. Rasmuson. *Banking on Alaska, the Story of the National Bank of Alaska, a History of NBA,* Vol. I. Anchorage: National Bank of Alaska, 2000.

Cotten, Bruce. *An Adventure in Alaska.* Baltimore: The Sun Printing Office, 1922.

Dall, William Healy. "On Masks, Labrets, and Certain Aboriginal Customs: with an Inquiry into the Bearing of Their Geographical Distribution." In *U.S. Bureau of American Ethnology, 1881-82*. Washington, 1884.

Dall, William Healy. "Report on Coal and Lignite of Alaska." In *U.S. Geological Survey 17th Annual Report, 1895-96, Part 1*. U.S. Geological Survey, 1896.

Davis, Nancy Yaw. "English Bay: History and Continuity." Manuscript. Anchorage: Cultural Dynamics, Ltd., September, 1987.

Davis, Neil. "Fata Morgana." Alaska Science Nuggets. Fairbanks: Geophysical Institute, University of Alaska Fairbanks, 1984.

De Armond, R. N. *The Founding of Juneau*. Juneau: Gastineau Channel Centennial Association, 1980.

De Laguna, Frederica. *The Archaeology of Cook Inlet, Alaska*. Anchorage: Alaska Historical Society, 1975.

Dixon, George. *A Voyage Round the World; But More Particularly to the North-West Coast of America: Performed in 1785, 1786, 1787, and 1788 in the King George and Queen Charlotte, Captains Portlock and Dixon*. London: G. Goulding, 1789.

Dorr, John A., Jr. "Tertiary Non-Marine Vertebrates in Alaska—the Lack Thereof." In *Bulletin of the American Association of Petroleum Geologists*, Vol. 48, No. 7, 1964.

Elliott, Henry W. *Our Arctic Province, Alaska and the Seal Islands*. New York: Charles Scribner's Sons, 1886.

Fagan, Brian. *The Little Ice Age, How Climate Made History, 1300-1850*. New York: Basic Books, 2000.

Fedorova, Svetlana G. *The Russian Population in Alaska and California, Late 18th Century–1867*. Translated and edited by Richard A. Pierce and Alton S. Donnelly. Ontario: The Limestone Press, 1973.

Field, Carmen and Coowe Walker. "A Site Profile of the Kachemak Bay Research Reserve: A Unit of the National Estuarine Research Reserve System." Homer: Kachemak Bay Research Reserve, 2003.

Fienup-Riordan, Ann. *The Living Tradition of Yup'ik Masks: Agayuliyararput, Our Way of Making Prayer*. Seattle: University of Washington Press, 1996.

Georgeson, C.C. "Annual Report of the Alaska Agricultural Experiment Stations for 1901." In *Annual Report of the Office of Experiment Stations for The Year Ended June 30, 1901*. U.S. Department of Agriculture, 1902.

Griffin, Joy, compiler. *Alaska 1964–Where Were You?* Homer: Wizard Works, 1996.

Hanscom, Dick. *Alaska and Yukon Stocks and Bonds*. Fairbanks: Alaska Rare Coins, 2002.

Higginson, Ella. *Alaska, the Great Country.* New York: The Macmillan Company, 1909.

Hinckley, Ted C. *Alaskan John G. Brady, Missionary, Businessman, Judge, and Governor, 1878-1918.* Miami: Miami University and Ohio State University Press, 1982.

Huston, John Robert. "A Geographical Analysis of the Fur Farming Industry in Alaska." Master's thesis, Berkeley, University of California, 1956.

Jacobsen, Johan A. *Alaskan Voyage, 1881-1883: An Expedition to the Northwest Coast of North America.* Translated by Erna Gunther. Chicago: University of Chicago Press, 1977.

Janson, Lone. *Those Alaska Blues.* Anchorage: Alaska Historical Commission, 1985.

Johnson, Hugh A. and Robert J. Coffman. "Land Occupancy: Ownership and Use on Homesteads in the Kenai Peninsula, Alaska 1955." Palmer: Alaska Agricultural Experiment Station, Bulletin 21, 1956.

Kachemak Bay Broadcasting, Inc. The Coffee Table, Interview with Pioneers Lee Clendenen, Helen March, Wilma Williams, Steve Zawistowski. Homer, May 12, 1993.

——. The Coffee Table. Discussion between Bill Newman and Janet Klein. Homer, July 30, 1994.

Kachemak Bay Research Reserve and National Oceanic and Atmospheric Administration, Coastal Services Center. Kachemak Bay Ecological Characterization. "Ecosystem Description—Physical Environment, Subduction and Seismicity." CD-ROM. NOAA/CSC/ 20017-CD. Charleston, SC: NOAA Coastal Services Center, 2001.

Kalifornsky, Peter. A Dena'ina Legacy: K'tl'egh'l Sukdu, the Collected Writings of Peter Kalifornsky. Edited by James Kari and Alan Boraas. Fairbanks: Alaska Native Language Center, 1991.

Kari, James. Dena'ina Topical Dictionary. Fairbanks: Alaska Native Language Center, 2007.

Kari, James and Priscilla Russell Kari. Dena'ina Elnena, Tanaina Country. Fairbanks: Alaska Native Language Center, 1982.

Karlstrom, Thor N. V. "Quaternary Geology of the Kenai Lowland and Glacial History of the Cook Inlet Region, Alaska." U.S. Geological Survey Professional Paper 443, 1964.

Kilbuck, John. The Yup'ik Eskimos As Described in the Travel Journals and Ethnographic Accounts of John and Edith Kilbuck Who Served with the Alaska Mission of the Moravian Church 1886-1900. Edited by Ann Fienup-Riordan. Kingston, Ontario: Limestone Press, 1988.

Kizzia, Tom. Series on Fox River Flats, Kachemak Bay. Homer News, Jan. 14-Feb 4, 1982.

Klein, Janet. *A History of Kachemak Bay, the Country, the Communities.* Homer: Homer Society of Natural History, 1981.

———. *Archaeology of Kachemak Bay, Alaska.* Homer: Kachemak Country Publications, 1995.

———. *Homer Spit, Coal, Gold and Con Men.* Homer: Kachemak Country Publications, 1996.

———. "Abandoned Villages, Discovered Histories." Paper prepared for the Alaska Humanities Forum, Anchorage, and the Chenik Institute, Homer, 1999.

———. *Celebrating Homer's Buildings.* Homer: Kachemak Country Publications, 2002.

Klein, Janet R. and Peter Zollars. "Radiocarbon Dates from the Early Holocene Component of a Stratified Site (SEL-009) at Aurora Lagoon, Kenai Peninsula, Alaska." In *Alaska Journal of Anthropology.* Vol. 1-2. Anchorage: Alaska Anthropological Association, 2004.

Kleinleder, Rich, David Erikson, Carmen Field, Conrad Field, Dale Chorman, Karl Stoltzfus and George West. "Checklist of Birds of Kachemak Bay, Alaska." Homer: Center for Alaskan Coastal Studies, 2006.

Kutchin, Howard M. "Report on the Salmon Fisheries of Alaska, 1901." Washington, D.C., 1902.

Langille, W. A. "The Proposed Forest Reserve on the Kenai Peninsula Alaska." U.S. Department of Agriculture, October-December, 1904.

Leer, Jeff, compiler. "Kenai Peninsula Alutiiq Place Name List." Typed list with handwritten additions. Fairbanks: Alaska Native Language Center, 1980.

Mathews, Donna and Barbara Sweetland Smith. *Science under Sail, Russia's Great Voyages to America, 1728-1867.* Anchorage: Anchorage Museum of History and Art, 2000.

McClintock Land Survey and Planning Company. "Port Graham." For The Kenai Peninsula Borough. National Oceanic and Atmospheric Administration and State of Alaska, June, 1989.

Middleton, John. *Clothing in Colonial Russian America: A New Look.* Alaska History No. 44. Fairbanks and Kingston, Ontario: The Limestone Press, 1996.

Naske, Claus-M. *Paving Alaska's Trails, the Work of the Alaska Road Commission.* Alaska Historical Commission Studies in History No. 152. Lanham, MD: University Press of America, 1986.

153

National Trust, The. *Rufford Old Hall.* London: The National Trust, 1998.

Olson, Wallace M. *Through Spanish Eyes: The Spanish Voyages to Alaska, 1774-1792.* Auke Bay, Alaska: Heritage Research, 2002.

Orth, Donald J. *Dictionary of Alaska Place Names.* U.S. Geological Survey Professional Paper 567, 1967.

Osgood, Cornelius. *The Ethnography of the Tanaina.* New Haven: Yale University Publications in Anthropology No. 16, 1976.

Pedersen, Elsa. *Kachemak Bay Years, an Alaska Homesteader's Memoir.* Walnut Creek: Hardscratch Press, 2001.

Pedersen, Elsa and Richard A. Pierce. "Port Axel, a Proposed Finnish Colony on Kachemak Bay." Anchorage: The Alaska Journal, Spring, 1976.

Pierce, Richard A. "The Russian Coal Mine on the Kenai." Anchorage: The Alaska Journal, Spring, 1975.

Pierce, Richard A. and Alexander Doll. "Alaskan Treasure, Our Search for the Russian Plates." Anchorage: The Alaska Journal, Winter, 1970.

Pioneers of Alaska, Igloo 32, Auxiliary 14. *In Those Days–Alaska Pioneers of the Lower Kenai Peninsula.* Homer: Pioneers of Alaska, 1991.

Rainwater, Chris. "A Short History of Livestock Grazing on the Fox River Flats." Unpublished paper. Homer: Natural Resources Conservation Service, n.d.

Rennick, Penny, editor. *Prehistoric Alaska.* Anchorage: Alaska Geographic, 1994.

Ricks, Melvin B. *Directory of Alaska Postoffices and Postmasters.* Ketchikan: Tongass Publishing Company, 1965.

Rounsefell, George A. "Contributions to the Biology of the Pacific Herring, *Clupea Pallasii,* and the Condition of the Fishery in Alaska." Washington, D.C.: Bulletin of the Bureau of Fisheries, Document No. 1080, 1930.

Scudder, H. C. "The Alaska Salmon Trap: Its Evolution, Conflicts, and Consequences." Juneau: Alaska State Library Historical Monograph No. 1, 1970.

Sherwood, Morgan. "A North Pacific Bubble, 1902-1907." Anchorage: Alaska History, Vol. 12, No. 1, 1997.

Skud, B.E., H.M. Sakuda and G.M. Reid. "Statistics of the Alaska Herring Fishery 1878-1956." U.S. Fish and Wildlife Service, 1960.

Soberg, Ralph. *Bridging Alaska, from the Big Delta to the Kenai.* Walnut Creek: Hardscratch Press, 1991.

Solovjova, Katerina G. and Aleksandra A. Vovnyanko. *The Fur Rush.* Translated by Richard L. Bland and Katya S. Wessels. Anchorage: Phenix Press, 2002.

Springer, Susan Woodward. *Seldovia Alaska, an Historical Portrait of Life in Herring Bay.* Littleton, Colorado: Blue Willow, Inc., 1997.

Stone, Ralph W. Unpublished field notes. Menlo Park: U.S. Geological Survey, 1904.

Tebenkov, Mikhail. *Atlas of the Northwest Coasts of America. Chart V.* Translated by Richard A. Pierce. Kingston, Ontario: Limestone Press, 1981.

Trasky, Lance. "Kachemak Bay—the Richest Bay in the World?" Alaska Fish Tales and Game Trails, Vol. 14, No. 2, Spring, 1982.

Waller, Roger M. and Kirk W. Stanley. *The Alaska Earthquake, March 27, 1964: Effects on Communities. Effects of the Earthquake of March 27, 1964 in the Homer Area, Alaska.* U.S. Geological Survey Professional Paper 542-D, 1968.

Westward Alaskan. "Mrs. Woodard Dies in Seward." Vol. 1, No. 4. Seldovia, Alaska, Aug. 18, 1936.

Williamson, F. W. Official Plat of Township #6 South, Range #13 West (Homer) of the Seward Meridian, Alaska. Survey accepted July 15, 1918. Anchorage: Government Land Office (Bureau of Land Management), 1918.

Williamson, F. W. Official Plat of Township #5 South, Range #15 West (Anchor Point) of the Seward Meridian, Alaska. Survey accepted May 5, 1919. Anchorage: Government Land Office (Bureau of Land Management), 1919.

Wolfe, Jack A. "Tertiary Plants from the Cook Inlet Region, Alaska." U.S. Geological Survey Professional Paper 398-B, 1966.

Wolfe, Jack A., D. M. Hopkins and Estella B. Leopold. "Tertiary Stratigraphy and Paleobotany of the Cook Inlet Region, Alaska." U.S. Geological Survey Professional Paper 398-A, 1966.

Woodman, Lyman L. *Duty Station Northwest, the U. S. Army in Alaska and Western Canada, 1867-1987.* Vol. 1. Anchorage: Alaska Historical Society, 1996.

Workman, William B. "Archaeology of the Southern Kenai Peninsula," Arctic Anthropology, Vol. 35, No. 1. Madison: University of Wisconsin Press, 1998.

Znamenski, Andrei A. *Through Orthodox Eyes: Russian Missionary Narratives of Travels to the Dena'ina and Ahtna, 1850s-1930s.* Fairbanks: University of Alaska Press, 2003.

INDEX

(Page numbers referring to illustrations are in italics.)